THE KITCHEN TABLE MILLIONAIRE

THE KITCHEN TABLE MILLIONAIRE

*Home-Based Money-Making Strategies
to Build Financial Independence Today*

Patrick Cochrane

PRIMA PUBLISHING

PRIMA PUBLISHING and colophon are registered trademarks of Prima Communications, Inc.

Library of Congress Cataloging-in-Publication Data
Cochrane, Patrick W.
The kitchen table millionaire : home-based money-making strategies to build financial independence today / Patrick W. Cochrane
  p. cm.
Includes index.
ISBN 0-7615-0929-1
1. Home-based businesses—Management. 2. New business enterprises. I. Title.
HD62.38.C63 1997
658'.041—dc21   96-47778
                                                            CIP

97 98 99 00 01 HH 10 9 8 7 6 5 4 3 2
Printed in the United States of America

HOW TO ORDER
Single copies may be ordered from Prima Publishing, P.O. Box 1260BK, Rocklin, CA 95677; telephone (916) 632-4400. Quantity discounts are available. On your letterhead, include information concerning the intended use of the books and the number of books you wish to purchase.

Visit us online at http://www.primapublishing.com

CONTENTS

PART THREE: MILLION-DOLLAR HOME-BASED BUSINESSES

PART FOUR: PROTECTING YOUR ASSETS

CHAPTER 16

FINANCIAL FLOURISH: KEEP YOUR BANKER FROM ROBBING YOU BLIND   187

INTRODUCTION

Too many people are thinking of security instead of opportunity. They seem more afraid of life than death.

James F. Byrnes

MOST AMERICANS ARE TOO BUSY scraping out a living from month to month to recognize where they really are in life. It's been said that many people quit working when they find a job. Yet we're literally killing ourselves to make a living. We've been misled to believe that the only way of achieving financial independence is to work for someone else. This may have been true in the fifties or sixties, but things are frighteningly different today. There's no need to go into the statistics on unemployment, homelessness, crime, and domestic violence; it's right there on the streets and in the media, staring us in the face every day.

Dragging yourself to a job you hate just for the money is about as far from success as you can get. You're still a slave to the system, no matter how much money you earn. What's the point of clawing your way up the ladder of success, only to find that it's leaning against the wrong wall? Even if you win the rat race, you're still a rat. There must be something better, right? There is, my friend, as you are about to discover.

Advanced technology has resulted in a growing number of jobs being either farmed out to independent contractors or eliminated entirely. Furthermore, the ranks of Americans approaching retirement far outnumber the work force needed to support them. Social Security is sinking in a swamp of inescapable debt. When the risk of being an employee is weighed against the risk of starting an independent home-based business, it's no wonder people are flocking to the latter in record numbers.

Successful entrepreneurs are not exceptionally well educated, gifted, or lucky. They are average, everyday individuals who decided to forsake the frustration and uncertainty of the present job market and make an absolute commitment to take control of their own destinies. They come from the ranks of the middle class, single parents, veterans, professionals, retirees, and welfare recipients. Their defining characteristics are dedication and resilience. They accept setbacks as part of the price to be paid for long-term success, and they know that the only sure way to overcome the fear of something new is to do it. This is where confidence lives. The major-league batting champion fails in more than 60 percent of his at-bats. For every home run Babe Ruth hit, he struck out twice. World championship teams lose forty to fifty games during the season. Life as an entrepreneur mirrors life in baseball: the emphasis isn't so much on winning as it is on learning to endure losing!

You'll never need to gamble on "get-rich-quick" schemes or drag yourself to another dubious seminar again. Thanks to the proven strategies revealed in this program, your risk has been almost entirely eliminated. If you make the effort to put these strategies into action, you *will* succeed. It's as simple as that. The majority of people spend their lives in search of a financial genie in a magic lamp to make their dreams come true. In the real world, it just isn't going to happen. Stephen Crane said it best: "A man said to the universe, 'Sir, I exist.' 'However,' replied the universe, 'the fact has not created in me a sense of obligation.'"

Those who fail to aggressively pursue their dreams are usually *deficiency motivated,* or focused on what is missing from their lives. In order to succeed, we must become *prosperity conscious,* or focused on what we are capable of achieving, even in the face of disappointment. As Ralph Waldo Emerson aptly put it, "You are what you think about, all day long." This program is designed to give you the necessary tools with which to forge an exciting new future, filled with limitless freedom, security, and prosperity. However, all the knowledge in the world is useless without a plan of action. In the end, your results will be directly proportionate to your efforts.

No matter what you do with your life, the value you receive will always be equal to the value you extend to others. The more value given, the more received. Money is merely the measure of the value you create that other people are willing to pay for. By examining your values and abilities and aligning them with your goals, you will find an idea, product, or service that can be produced inexpensively and sold on a value-for-value basis.

Imagine of the power and satisfaction that come from earning a comfortable living doing something you truly love and are passionate about. That's the philosophy of this book: achieving financial independence through a natural extension of your individual abilities, talents, or even hobbies. Most wealthy people love their work, not just for the money, but because they are living their passion. When you align your values with your goals they become the same, and you will prosper beyond your wildest expectations. It will simply become inevitable.

It all starts with a decision. When you write down the reasons why you want to achieve your goals, you'll create the motivation and commitment to make them happen. This means severing your umbilical cord to the past and taking the necessary steps toward achieving your goals. You become successful the moment you take the leap from a dream to a vision with the power of decision. A deliberate, well-planned decision leads to wealth, happiness, and contentment. Indecision leads to stress, fear, and failure. Successful people refuse to rely on fate, luck, or other people to tell them who and what they should be; they go out and make it happen.

Keys to Prosperity

Starting now, you can put to work the fundamentals for achieving affluence in your life. This is the foundation upon which you will build your business. When you have a firm grasp on these basic principles, you'll feel more confident and inspired to get started.

1. Align your values and abilities with your goals.
2. Create a product or service that provides value for others.
3. Target the widest possible consumer market.
4. Effectively deliver your message.
5. Under-promise and over-deliver in your customer service.
6. Enjoy your success and live your dreams.

The keys to the Ferrari are in your hands. It's time to unleash the fierce entrepreneurial spirit and unshakable determination that dwell within you. Expect skepticism from your family and friends. In fact, thrive on it. After all, if financial success came in a bottle at Macy's, everyone would be a millionaire!

Extraordinary Success Stories of Ordinary People

The best way to illustrate the wealth power of everyday ideas is through examples of people just like you who have transformed their ideas to action. I find it invigorating to discover stories of good old American ingenuity in action. Here are some of their inspiring stories. I hope they provide a spark to get you started on that long-dormant brainstorm you've been meaning to get around to.

CHOCO-LOGOS

A California woman makes chocolates in the shape of corporate and company logos. She got started by gathering business addresses from her local Chamber of Commerce and Yellow Pages, then followed up with a sales letter. This is a six-figure-a-year business with a product that's in constant demand.

CAT'S MEOW

You may have seen that cute poster of a cat hanging from a bamboo pole, with the caption "Hang In There, Baby." What began as an spontaneous shot of a photographer's pet Siamese cat sold 25,000 copies in only a few months. The photographer originally marketed the poster by mail, but he was so swamped with orders that he needed twenty distributors to handle the volume!

STEP-FAMILY GREETING CARDS

A New Jersey woman who grew tired of having to insert the word "step" into greeting cards created a company called "Stepfolk Greeting Cards." Her products are currently available in card shops across the country, earning several hundred thousand dollars a year in royalties.

DIAPER DIVA

A Los Angeles woman founded "Call Mother Goose" to deliver a variety of baby products—from diapers to bottled formula—right to the homes of harried mothers. Prices are about 15 percent higher than in stores, but she knew that customers wouldn't mind paying a little extra for the convenience. Awareness of the business is spread largely by word of mouth. "Call Mother Goose" grossed $250,000 in its first year of operation.

CAMCORDER CASH

A Chicago barber was inundated with orders (at $29.95 a pop) to videotape baby's first haircut. He makes more from the video than from the haircut.

PET PASSPORTS

Using the same color and design that are used in genuine passports, a California entrepreneur developed a product that allows pet lovers to document details of their animal's care, feeding, identification, and vaccination history. Since selling the idea to a pet store chain, over 40,000 units have been sold nationwide at six dollars each!

T-SHIRTS OF THE TIMES

You see them everywhere: hustling entrepreneurs selling T-shirts and novelty items with clever slogans, and turning an after-costs profit of 300 percent or more. If you're on the ball and get involved early enough, the latest fad or scandal can reap a windfall of quick cash.

CONFIDENTIAL SKIVVIES

A grandmother from Houston recognized a need among businessmen to purchase exotic lingerie for their wives or girlfriends without the embarrassment of going into a boutique. By holding fashion shows in bars and hotels, Grandma grossed over $100,000 in sales in her first year.

SAME AS ABOVE, WITH A TWIST

A New York businesswoman runs a mail-order Panty-of-the-Month Club, offering perfumed designer panties that she acquires wholesale from France. Packaged in a ribboned, gold-sealed envelope with a personal note, and priced at $16.50 a month, she grossed $160,000 within the first year, with projected sales of $300,000 for the second.

LONG-STEM COOKIES

Mail-order mania strikes again. A Utah woman ships packages containing a dozen chocolate-chip cookies with a floral stem pushed through the middle. She started the business by advertising in in-flight airline magazines, taking orders by phone, and shipping by UPS. The result? Forty thousand dollars in sales the first year, with projected sales of $80,000 the next.

OLLIE NORTH COULD HAVE USED THIS

A San Jose woman operates Mobile Shredding Company, a paper shredder on wheels. Recognizing the needs of banks, high-tech companies, and law firms to dispose of sensitive or classified documents, she has a list of 180 clients who pay an hourly rate of fifty dollars. She grosses a tidy $180,000 annually.

Overcoming Fear and Failure

"It's not whether you win or lose, but how you play the game." That's fine if you're in kindergarten, but it's suicide in the business world where success is measured by *results*. If you don't think of the future, you won't have one. You can or be acted *upon*. It's that simple. Wouldn't you rather control your life than just react to it?

A certain amount of fear is healthy; it forces you to deal with challenges and face problems head-on. But you can't allow fear to paralyze you and make you susceptible to negativity—your own or that of your family and friends. People around you may be fearful and jealous of your ambition without consciously realizing it. Ambrose Bierce said, "Success is the one unpardonable sin against one's fellows." Many are intimidated by those who attempt to turn dreams into reality, because they are unwilling to venture beyond the dream stage themselves. You must:

1. Clearly *define* your goals.
2. Develop an unshakable *desire* to achieve those goals.
3. Take *action* in the face of *fear* to make your goals become reality.

Entrepreneurs are disappointed, but never discouraged, by failure. They use setbacks as learning experiences, analyzing their role in the failure and figuring out how to avoid similar problems in the future. Because the entrepreneur is competitive and passionate about success, he or she will do whatever it takes to make it happen. This includes constantly seeking out feedback and information in order to improve. Here are some tips to help develop your entrepreneurial skills and bolster your chances of success:

- Establish relationships with personal advisors such as a lawyer and an accountant.
- Learn from your mistakes and develop your planning and management skills. Learning about business operations is an ongoing process. Local community colleges offer inexpensive short courses on business-related

POWERTIP

The Open University was founded in 1987 by Lawrence J. Pino to provide training and skills to self-employed entrepreneurs. Based in Orlando, Florida, it is the only accredited institution of its kind. For information, contact The Open University, 24 South Orange Avenue, Orlando, FL 32801; (708) 291-1616.

subjects such as "Financing For Small Business" and "Small Business Bookkeeping."
- Establish a network of small-business owners with similar interests, needs, and problems. Feedback from others is a great way to avoid mistakes and to benefit from shared experience.
- Subscribe to industry trade magazines and newsletters (there are a wealth of them listed in this book). Use them to expose your product or service to other business owners.

Rejection is part of the human experience and failure is inevitable. While both may sting momentarily, they can't hurt you. Successful entrepreneurs accept rejection, yet remain determined to plow through until they win acceptance. Some effective confidence boosters are:

- Believe in yourself.
- Forgive yourself for mistakes, heal, and move forward.
- Use logic to overcome negative emotions.

There is an abundance of information available on every subject you can think of. Thanks to computers, direct mail, the news media, and the telephone, this information is easier to access than it ever has been. The more proficient you become at gathering the information you need, the more successful you will be.

THE KITCHEN TABLE
MILLIONAIRE

PART ONE

Getting Started

CHAPTER 1

TURNING YOUR IDEAS INTO WEALTH

*An idea isn't worth much
until someone with dedication
makes it happen.*

William Feather

IN THE MOVIE COCKTAIL, Tom Cruise is lounging with Elisabeth Shue at a poolside bar in the Bahamas, his gaze fixed on the little umbrella that adorns his drink. "Y'know, some guy sold a million of these things and got rich," he muses.

We've all been fascinated by the simple ideas that have made people wealthy. Look around you right now. Everything you see was once an idea floating around in someone's head—probably several people's heads. But only those who took action on their ideas reaped the rewards. Some people came along with an improvement or a slight variation on an original idea and made a fortune. The inventor of the colored paper clip made more money than the inventor of the original paper clip!

How many times have you had a great idea that died because you didn't know just how easily you could turn it into profit? You don't have to be Einstein to be an inventor; everyday interests, annoyances, and inconveniences are all opportunities in disguise. If it affects you, chances are it affects others, too. This is the sign of a potential market for your idea.

Products that make people healthier, wealthier, sexier, or less stressed can make you rich. The same goes for even the slightest variations that make existing products better, faster, cheaper, or more convenient. Many people dismiss their ideas as frivolous or silly—or assume that someone else has already thought of them. They believe the process of capitalizing on their ideas is more complicated and expensive than it really is. If this sounds like you, read on.

Almost everyone has had an idea or an inspiration that, with the proper motivation and resources, can be marketed successfully. The secret is to harness those bursts of inspiration and creativity. Don't just dismiss them with a shrug or an excuse. Explore the possibilities and tune in to possibilities you hadn't considered. When an idea comes to you, don't let it slip away; hit the brakes and write it down. Keep casual, informal notes.

There are two kinds of thinking: analytical and creative. Analytical thinking involves using proven formulas or past experiences to arrive at a solution. Creative thinking involves brainstorming: putting things together in new or unorthodox ways. Creative thinking is the process that can lead you to that million-dollar idea. *Miracle Mop*, *The Club*, and the *Abdomenizer* are all the result of creative thinking. The best way to initiate the brainstorming process is to quickly write down any and all ideas that come to you, without stopping to evaluate or criticize them. When you're finished brainstorming you can analyze and organize the information. This is how many innovative ideas are born.

You'll be amazed at how ridiculously easy it is to develop an idea and pitch it to a manufacturer (who does all the work for you), then relax and collect a royalty from each sale. Let's look at some ordinary people who took action and made a fortune from their ideas. The Pet Rock made Gary Dahl a millionaire in only three months. Woodie Hall took the "Happy Face" craze one step further by simply painting it onto a Ping-Pong ball, and sold 500,000 units within ninety days. Since 1968, Woodie has placed over 150 of his novelties and games with manufacturers. At an average retail price of five dollars per item, Woodie has made a fortune from his 5 percent royalties! Now over eighty years old, he continues to churn out ideas in the workshop of his lakefront dream home in Southern California.

Finding Your Product or Service

Common sense is your most valuable tool in choosing your vehicle on the path to success. Here are some issues you should think about as you decide.

PICK A GROWING FIELD OF OPPORTUNITY

A new field of play is more level than an established one. It's more difficult to keep up with competitors who have a head start on you. Read, research, and stay on top of new trends and paradigm shifts in the marketplace. If you stay on your toes, you'll be in position to identify and act on new opportunities.

FILL AN UNMET NEED

When you discover a new trend, chances are there will already be someone there. Tap into an existing demand. Find out what the competition is doing and, more importantly, what they're *not* doing, and focus in that direction.

KNOW WHEN TO MOVE ON

Life cycles of products and services are getting shorter all the time. You need to stay on top of rapidly changing customer demand. Obtain industry and customer feedback, and constantly look for improvements and new opportunities. Ride the wave to its crest, then move on to the next challenge.

HONE IN ON YOUR IDEA

To determine whether your product or service is a potential winner, ask yourself four important questions (hint: the answer to numbers two through four should be *yes*):

1. What does it do?
2. Do people need it?
3. Does it solve a problem or enrich people's lives?
4. Does it improve on an existing product?

Here are some of the best areas for new product ideas:

- toys, games, novelty items
- posters, T-shirts, hats
- home improvements
- automobiles/driving
- recreation and leisure
- protection/security devices
- child safety

Toys and novelties are a good place to get started, since these items tend to remain on the market for an average of one year. Hot sellers may be around even longer. Make sure your idea is inexpensive to produce; between five and eight dollars is ideal. Remember, the goal is volume sales. The more you sell, the bigger the royalty check. Make sure there's a market for your idea. Put together a sketch, drawing, or prototype. Don't sweat the details. The goal is to attract interest in your idea, while simultaneously protecting it until you can make a deal with a manufacturer. The standard way to protect your idea is with a "Proof of Invention" form. But more on that later.

FIVE STEPS FOR TURNING YOUR IDEA INTO INCOME

1. Develop it.
2. Test it on family and friends.
3. Build a model or prototype.
4. Protect it.
5. Price, package, and promote it!

Common Excuses That Kill Great Ideas

Here are some of the excuses people make for not acting on their ideas:

"I'M NOT SMART ENOUGH TO INVENT SOMETHING NEW"

Hogwash. Unless you've been living on Pluto, you have the same faculties to experience life as anyone else. Jerry Seinfeld explains that his ability to find humor in "nothing," is based on the fact that he has developed the capacity to see situations he's involved in as an observer—as though he were watching things from the ceiling in a corner of the room. Everyday routines hold inspiration and possibilities. It's simply a matter of sharpening your powers of observation.

Pay attention to the nuances of everyday life: showering, shaving, cooking, cleaning, driving, playing, loving . . . living. Supermarkets, novelty stores, auto shops, and amusement parks are all places to find ways of improving on an existing product or idea. You may not even need to leave the house to find the idea that can make you rich. It all begins by recognizing and developing your powers of observation.

"IT'S ALREADY BEEN DONE"

Don't let paranoia overcome you. No matter how similar, no two concepts ever hit the market identically. Otherwise, there would only be one model of car, one chain of burger joints, one kind of beer. There's always room for a new twist or slant on an existing idea.

"BUT I'M NOT A SALESPERSON"

Sorry. Everyone is a salesperson, like it or not. When you apply for a job, you're selling yourself to the employer, and when you apply for a mortgage or car financing, you're selling the company on your willingness and ability to repay the loan. All you need is the motivation, the desire for prosperity, and the basic methodology with which to sell your idea or product.

"I DON'T KNOW ANYTHING ABOUT PATENTS OR MARKETING"

The true brilliance of inventing is its simplicity. If a manufacturing company accepts your idea, it can handle everything. This includes patent searches (to make sure no one else has already invented your idea), production, and marketing (getting it onto store shelves). You receive either a lump-sum payment or a royalty on every unit sold.

"WHAT IF I GET RIPPED OFF BY THE MANUFACTURER?"

Manufacturers earn their living by producing ideas, not stealing them. Since new ideas are their lifeblood, it would be professional suicide to exploit inventors. You're far more likely to be taken by an "invention marketing" company. Many of these operations have come under fire from the Federal Trade Commission for making false or unrealistic promises with respect to their ability (and intent) to honestly represent their clients' products. The best way to market your idea is to deal directly with a manufacturer. You'll not only avoid the risk of dealing with unscrupulous operators, but you'll keep your entire royalty instead of splitting it with a third party.

Naming Your Product

Avoid gimmicks; create a descriptive, catchy title that is easy to remember and illustrates what the product is. Advertising buzzwords like "Miracle," "Revolutionary," "Amazing," and "New and Improved" are used over and over because they work.

If your product does something unique, try to incorporate it into the title. For example, those who work with tools know that *Metwrench* is a metric wrench. Simple, yet effective. This also goes for naming a company. A name like "Toys 'R' Us" leaves very little doubt as to what the company sells.

Protecting Your Idea

Perhaps the easiest way to protect your idea is to write down a short description of your concept. Make two copies, and mail one to your lawyer and one to yourself. The postmark is your protection. Keep the envelope sealed for certification.

> **POWERTIP**
>
> **Inventors online.** On this valuable e-mail list, discussions include everything from developing your ideas and obtaining patents to licensing and marketing strategies. To subscribe, send e-mail to *listserv@home.ease.lsoft.com*. Just type "subscribe inventors [your name]" in both the subject field and body of the message.

POWERTIP

You can receive a free thirty-minute consultation with a patent attorney through the Intellectual Property Law Association's Inventor Consultation Service. For information, contact:

**The American Intellectual
Property Law Association**
2001 Jefferson Davis Highway, Suite 203
Arlington, VA 22202

Another form of preliminary protection is known as a "disclosure document." This protects your idea for the first two years while you generate revenue for a patent-pending application, patent search, and patent or trademark. To file a disclosure document, send copies of blueprints, photos, illustrations, and supporting documentation along with ten dollars and a self-addressed, stamped envelope to:

The Commissioner of Patents and Trademarks
Washington, DC 20231

Trademarks, Patents, Copyrights, and ISBNs

It is very wise to safeguard your hard work by obtaining the appropriate protections. In general, Intellectual Property Rights include:

1. Patents: protect an invention
2. Trademarks: protect a logo, name, or motto for a product
3. Copyrights: protect an original artistic or literary work
4. Trade Secrets: protect the details of a product to prevent knockoffs

And, if you are writing a literary work, it is also a good idea to file for an International Standard Book Number (ISBN), which will become its signature identification for the life of the book.

PATENTS

A patent provides an inventor with the exclusive right to prevent others from trespassing on an invention for the life of a valid patent. In order to obtain a patent, an invention must be new, innovative, not obvious, and, of course, useful. Obtaining a patent is an expensive, frustrating process that can take up to three years. A patent does not guarantee either protection or marketing success. A patent is awarded to the individual who not only had the original idea, but who actively pursued it.

Once you have published or marketed your idea, you have one year to apply for a patent. United States patents are only valid in this country, so if you're considering foreign markets, you may require the services of a patent attorney to start the necessary paperwork even before you begin marketing in the U.S.

A patent is no guarantee against infringements or rip-offs. There are outfits that do nothing but copy successful products and ideas. Your only recourse is to file suit; this is expensive and time-consuming, and you never know which way the scales of justice are going to tip. Damages against a patent infringer do not begin until you've actually been issued a patent. The purpose of a patent is to discourage others from claiming ownership and/or competing with your idea. Therefore, a patent *application* can be even better than the patent itself (and a lot less expensive). If you own a patent, all the information is available to anyone who wants to see it, whereas a patent *pending* provides privacy in addition to protection, since your documentation doesn't become public record until the patent is granted. Don't bother with the time and expense of obtaining a patent until you're actually marketing your product.

COPYRIGHTS

A copyright prevents others from copying an original work, and can be used to protect a book, audio or video recording, computer software, etc. Copyrights are registered with the Library of Congress.

A copyright protects an author's ideas and form of expression, and lasts for the lifetime of the creator, or seventy-five years in the case of a work-for-hire. For information and copyright forms contact:

Copyright Office
Library of Congress
Washington, DC 20559
(202) 707-3000

TRADEMARKS

A trademark protects a word, phrase, symbol, or logo that identifies a product or service with its source of origin, and lasts as long as the trademark is in use. You must be sure that the mark is not a generic or descriptive name for the product or service, or a trademark may not be granted. For details, contact: U.S. Patent and Trademark Office: (703) 557-4636, or Trademark Assistance Center: (703) 308-9000.

TRADE SECRETS

A trade secret can cover any confidential information used in business that provides the possessor with a competitive advantage. All this does is (hopefully) prevent someone from stealing it. If someone comes up with the same idea as your trade secret, you have no course of action. However, if the idea is stolen, you have legal recourse.

The best way to leave your competitors in the dark is to keep your key manufacturing processes or materials to yourself. KFC and Coca-Cola are two companies that protect their recipes. The less information that is available, the more difficult it will be for someone to knock off your product or idea.

INTERNATIONAL STANDARD BOOK NUMBERS

If you are self-publishing a book, it is very important to obtain an International Standard Book Number (ISBN) for it. The ISBN provides instant data regarding your literary work (title, author, copyright, etc.), and is often incorporated into a bar code. To obtain an ISBN, contact R. R. Bowker at (908) 665-6770 or fax (908) 464-3553.

When you receive your ISBN, you'll need to incorporate it into your bar code. This costs about twenty-five dollars. Contact one of the bar-coding specialists listed in the Resource Directory. For books, specify that you want a Bookland EAN bar code with price extension.

Finding a Manufacturer

The best way to find a manufacturer for your product is to investigate existing products similar to your own. If you have an idea for a novelty item, go to a novelty store. Manufacturers' names and addresses are usually printed right on the packaging. If you've invented a new lamp, check out some lighting fixtures stores to see who makes them. Manufacturers can also be found in *McRae's Blue Book* or *Thomas' Register of American Manufacturers* in the reference section of your local library. *Thomas' Register* costs approximately $180, and is available directly from:

Thomas Publishing Company
One Penn Plaza, 26th Floor
New York, NY 10119
(212) 695-0500

Make a list of manufacturers that make products similar to yours, and contact them for an information package. Fill out their application forms completely, and explain your idea. What does it do? What makes it unique and valuable to the consumer? Be aggressive, and really sell the benefits and features.

Your application will probably include a Proof of Invention form, along with a blueprint or model of your idea. The Proof of Invention form is your protection when disclosing your idea to the manufacturer. Don't reveal every last specification and detail. Keep it simple. Show the form to your lawyer, and have it witnessed by two people (other than family members) and notarized. Make photocopies for your own records, and to send to other manufacturers if necessary.

PROTOTYPES

A manufacturer may request to see a prototype of your idea. There are three kinds of prototype:

1. *Working Model.* Not necessarily the final version, yet functional enough for demonstrations and testing.
2. *Preproduction Model.* Similar to the final version, but lacking the fine-tuning.
3. *Production Model.* The finished version that will be sold to consumers.

To create a prototype, locate manufacturers of prototypes and models in the Yellow Pages under "Designers, Industrial," "Inventors," and "Product Designers." You could even post a notice with a brief description of your product on the bulletin board at a local design school. Remember to protect your idea by obtaining a confidentiality agreement before proceeding.

ACCEPTANCE OR REJECTION

Within six to eight weeks, you should receive an evaluation form from the manufacturer advising you of two important things: whether your idea is original, and whether they're interested in developing it.

If your idea is rejected, the manufacturer will usually tell you why (no market for the product, too expensive to produce, etc.). The keys are patience and persistence. Charles Darrow's idea for Monopoly was initially rejected by Parker Brothers before they finally came around in 1935. The rest is history, with over seventy-five million sold to date.

The day you receive your first offer is very exciting! The manufacturer may request a demonstration of your idea, or offer suggestions regarding design modifications. They can also handle all the necessary paperwork to register your idea. They will offer either a contract to purchase or a royalty agreement. They will explain their marketing strategy from packaging to distribution. If a manufacturer offers to purchase your idea outright, as opposed to offering a royalty on sales, this could be an indication you have a potential mega-hit.

POWERTIP

The Dream Merchants is a trade magazine for inventors. For information, contact:

The Dream Merchants
2309 Torrance Boulevard, Suite 201
Torrance, CA 90501
(310) 328-1925

If this is the case, you'll have an important decision to make. Before selling out to a manufacturer for a flat fee (also known as the "dime-store" approach), do some market research. Demonstrate your idea to as many people as possible. This will give you an idea of your product's long-term potential. Even at 5 percent, the royalties can add up quickly. Microsoft made a dime-store deal and bought the original DOS software for less than $80,000, and Bill Gates turned it into a multi-billion-dollar empire! On the other hand, many ideas are purchased and never make it to market. Some companies buy out potential competitors just to secure their position in the market. If you decide to sell, stipulate that the rights to your idea will revert to you if the manufacturer fails to produce it within a certain amount of time. Or else make sure they cut you a *huge* check.

There's no greater satisfaction and thrill than the one you'll get from discovering and developing your unique, individual ideas. Instead of just reacting to life, you can start acting on your dreams. Placing a successful product on the market can give you an amazing buzz. You'll be immortalizing a part of yourself, and the royalty checks can keep rolling in for years. And, of course, success breeds confidence. You'll gain the valuable experience and motivation to create other unique products that will supply you with a lifetime income—with no limit to what you can achieve!

CHAPTER 2

LAYING THE FOUNDATION FOR SUCCESS

> *You can't build a reputation on what you're going to do.*
>
> **Henry Ford**

ONCE YOU HAVE DECIDED what kind of product or service to offer, the next step is to turn your dream into reality. In this chapter we'll explore how to set up your business as quickly and expediently as possible. I thought it would be fun to begin with some of the tax advantages of self-employment in order to excite and inspire you. Then we'll cover record keeping, tax forms, accountants, lawyers, types of businesses . . . you know, the boring stuff that all entrepreneurs hate, but have to deal with. Then we'll look at some of the basic equipment that can help you get established as quickly and painlessly as possible. But first, two essential starters:

One: Register Your Business

Start by opening a separate checking account for your business. This will eliminate much of the confusion surrounding taxes and record keeping. Visit your county clerk's office or your local office supply store and pick up a "doing business as" (DBA) form. You'll receive three copies. Fill out the forms, have them notarized, and register one copy with the county clerk's office. Use the second copy to open a bank account under your business name, and keep the third copy for your records. That's it. You're in business.

Two: Watch Your Spending

Avoid the temptation to go wild purchasing office furniture and fancy equipment until your business is up and running. Commit every available dollar to generating positive cash flow. In the words of Theodore Roosevelt, "Do what you can with what you have, where you are." Dreaming is safe; spending money is risky. When things begin to roll, you'll notice your business naturally evolving and forming itself.

Tax Advantages of a Home-Based Business

Owning a business offers some of the most extraordinary tax shelters available. You can legally write off a multitude of personal expenses that are unavailable to the average taxpayer. Have you ever wondered why the rich pay such minimal tax? Right or wrong, 74 percent of all American millionaires own their own businesses, enabling them to

---

POWERTIP

Information USA by Matthew Lesko, president of Washington Researchers, is available in bookstores and libraries. It provides a wealth of consumer information and sources on just about anything you can imagine. Washington Researchers also offers books, tapes, and directories containing information on a variety of government services, programs, grants, and free or low-cost government publications. For information contact:

Washington Researchers
2612 P Street NW
Washington, DC 20007
(202) 333-3499

write off a wide array of business-related expenses. The self-employed pay little or no withholding tax (which, in reality, is a free accounting service your employer provides to the IRS); instead, they pay quarterly tax payments, a more flexible system. Insurance, utilities, house-cleaning fees, maintenance, property taxes, and mortgage interest or rent are all legitimate home-business tax deductions.

To determine the percentage of your household expenses that you can take as a tax deduction, simply calculate the square footage of your home office as a percentage of the area of your entire home. If your office occupies 400 square feet of a 2,000-square-foot home, you can deduct twenty percent of the expenses mentioned above. (Be aware, however, that Congress is considering legislation that would require you to pay taxes on any home-office depreciation expenses you claimed in the past when you sell your home.)

As a home-based business owner, you automatically qualify for these benefits and more. The first step is to secure the services of a professional who specializes in home-based tax law, to ensure that you maintain proper records and are always up to date on any changes in legislation affecting your business. Why not take advantage of all the tax breaks you're entitled to? Here are some of the big ones:

YOUR HOME

You can deduct a percentage of your household costs based on the amount of space that you use exclusively and on a regular basis for your business (certified by letterhead, a log of your operations, a photograph of the office, etc.). This includes utilities, insurance, property tax, and mortgage interest. Portions of maintenance costs, including repairs, painting, and cleaning services, are also deductible. Office equipment (computer, fax, telephone, and answering machines) and office furniture—including depreciation—are deductible.

YOUR CAR

Keep a record of your mileage, as well as expenses such as gas and parking fees, relating to the use of your auto for business purposes only. A second vehicle that can be used exclusively for business travel would be ideal. Otherwise, you'll need separate records for business and personal use. You can buy an "auto expense log" at any office supply store. The IRS even allows you to deduct a certain amount of depreciation on the vehicle.

MEDICAL EXPENSES

Roughly 25 percent of health insurance premiums is tax-deductible. Although there are no specific deductions for medical expenses, if you're married you can deduct 100 percent of your health insurance premiums and medical expenses by hiring your spouse. You'll require a written medical plan and documentation from your insurance company certifying your spouse as an employee. Even though you aren't eligible, your spouse is. By choosing a health plan that includes the employee's spouse (you) and dependent children, you'll have 100 percent coverage. Just be sure to maintain accurate records documenting your spouse's legitimate employment in your business.

HIRING YOUR CHILDREN

A terrific way to divert tax funds to your kids is to hire them to run errands, stuff envelopes, clean your office, and so on. As long as the employment is genuine (pay them reasonable hourly wages by check only, and keep records of hours worked), wages earned by a child under the age of eighteen are exempt from Social Security and Medicare taxes. A dependent child also pays no tax on the first $3,700 of earned income, translating into savings of up to fifty percent of the total. You'll save another $2,000 by opening an IRA account for each child.

There are a multitude of deductions available to the home-based business person, from education costs and tax-deferred retirement accounts (Keoghs) all the way down to

POWERTIP
Wilkinson Benefit Consultants will analyze the three best health insurance policies to meet your needs. The cost is $270. Call (800) 296-3030.

business meals and vacations. The IRS allows you to combine a vacation with a business trip, as long as the trip is primarily business-related (seminars, trade shows, meetings with suppliers, etc.). In fact, you can even bring your spouse, and deduct the entire cost of a single hotel room as opposed to half the cost of a double.

RETIREMENT PLANS

Consider starting one of the following:

- A simplified employee pension (SEP) that allows you to shelter up to 13 percent of your net annual earnings (up to $22,500) if you are not incorporated, and after you've deducted half of your self-employment tax.
- An Individual Retirement Account (IRA); contribute $2,000 per year.
- One of two existing types of Keogh accounts. Consult your accountant for a complete, up-to-date range of available options.

Tax Forms and Record Keeping

Here are some of the government forms that apply to small businesses, available from your local IRS or Small Business Administration (SBA) office (see the Resource Directory):

- *Your Federal Income Tax* (Publication 17)
- *Tax Guide for Small Business* (Publication 334)
- *Business Use of Your Home* (Publication 334)
- *Self-Employment Tax* (Publication 533)
- *Tax Information on Depreciation* (Publication 534)
- *Information on Excise Taxes* (Publication 510)
- *Tax Withholding and Estimated Tax* (Publication 505)
- *Employer's Tax Guide* (Circular E)

Remember that every business decision, purchase, and transaction you make has tax implications or built-in advantages or disadvantages. Each situation is unique, and tax laws change constantly, so consult an attorney and/or accountant who can advise you on your individual obligations and benefits.

POWERTIP

The Small Business Survival Committee's monthly newsletter tracks legislation affecting home-based businesses. Annual subscriptions cost twenty-five dollars. For information, call (800) 223-7526.

Maintaining accurate and up-to-date business records is, for most entrepreneurs, one of the most uninteresting and tedious aspects of running a home-based business. Fortunately, options exist. Computer programs such as Peachtree Accounting and Quicken make basic record keeping a snap. Set up your bookkeeping system before you start your business. Always keep up-to-date records, especially if your business is related to an activity that might be considered a hobby. If the IRS challenges the validity of your business, you'll need comprehensive records in order to defend your tax deductions.

Your records should reflect the following three categories:

1. How much cash you owe.
2. How much cash you are due.
3. How much cash you have on hand.

Your Lawyer

In the best of circumstances you will never need the services of a lawyer. However, should the need arise, here are some tips to help make the process less intimidating. Some local bar associations run lawyer referral and information services. Some just give names, and others actually provide information on experience and fees to help match your needs to the lawyer's background and billing procedures. When evaluating a particular lawyer, ask for a resume and check references.

When you select a lawyer, let him or her know that you expect to be informed of all developments pertaining to your affairs and consulted before any decisions are made. Ask the lawyer to estimate the timetable and costs of your case. Place a ceiling on fees, after which the lawyer must inform you before proceeding with work that increases your bill.

Always get a written retainer agreement that describes what you and your lawyer expect from each other. You may also want to receive copies of all documents, letters, and memos written and received on your behalf, or arrange to read them in the lawyer's office. A lawyer should never negotiate on your behalf without your consent. An overzealous lawyer can cost you a business deal, a lawsuit, you name it. Instruct your lawyer to write only what is agreed on, and to consult you before introducing anything else. If there is a lawsuit, insist that the other party give his or her lawyer the same instructions. This will save you a lot of time and trouble down the line.

Your Accountant

Most businesses fail, not because of a lack of good ideas or hard work, but from a lack of financial expertise and planning. An accountant who specializes in small business can help you set up your books, draw up and analyze profit-and-loss statements, help with financial decisions, and provide advice on cash requirements for your start-up phase. He or she can make budget forecasts, help prepare financial information for loan applications, and handle tax-related matters. Most accounting firms will maintain books, prepare bank reconciliation statements, and design and implement the most efficient bookkeeping systems to fit your requirements.

Your accountant is your key financial advisor. He or she will alert you to potential danger areas and advise you on how to handle growth spurts and survive lean periods. Check the Yellow Pages under "Accounting and Bookkeeping" to find a professional who specializes in small or home-based business. Explain how your business is run and ask for references from similar clients so you can research potential accountants. Don't be intimidated by the prospect of enlisting professional expertise. It will easily pay for itself with the time you'll save to focus on the creative and operational aspects of your business instead of wasting your valuable time "counting beans."

POWERTIP

The Vest-Pocket Entrepreneur: Everything You Need to Start and Run Your Own Business will give you further insight into how to avoid business failure (see Resource Directory). Also included are tips on financial planning, accounting, and management. It is available for $17.95 from:

Prentice-Hall
P.O. Box 11071
Des Moines, IA 50366
(800) 947-7700

What Type of Business Is Right for You?

There are three basic categories of business structure to chose from:

1. Sole proprietorship
2. Partnership
3. Corporation

The type of business you choose depends on the following factors:

- Field of business
- Number of people involved in the business
- Intended distribution of profits
- Tax advantages or disadvantages
- Capital requirements
- Liabilities assumed
- Legal restrictions

Most home-based businesses are sole proprietorships, but you may benefit from other structures that are unique to your individual situation. The following guidelines may help you decide the type of business that's right for you.

SOLE PROPRIETORSHIP

This is the easiest, most inexpensive way to start a business. Starting a sole proprietorship is as easy as getting the necessary forms from the county clerk, checking zoning restrictions, and opening for business. Tax records are simple, since business profits are listed as general income on your tax return.

You can even do business using your personal checking account (although it's not a good idea). If your business is an unlikely target for lawsuits and you don't need to raise capital, a sole proprietorship may be the way to go.

Advantages

- Easiest to start
- Maximum freedom and control
- Optimum tax advantages

Disadvantages

- Unlimited liability
- Death or illness endangers business
- Growth dependent on personal performance
- Personal affairs easily mixed with business

PARTNERSHIP

A partnership can be formed with a simple oral agreement between two or more persons, but such informality is discouraged. Legal fees for a partnership agreement are higher than those for a sole partnership, but may be lower than for incorporating. It's a good idea to have a written partnership agreement that outlines each partner's responsibilities in order to help settle any disputes that may arise down the road.

Advantages

- Two heads are better than one
- Combined capital (two pockets are better than one)
- Perceived by banks as better credit risk than corporation of similar size

Disadvantages

- Unclear chain of command
- Difficult to get rid of bad partner
- Death, withdrawal, or bankruptcy of one partner can endanger business

CORPORATION

Incorporating offers distinct tax advantages, but can be more complicated and expensive to set up. The IRS scrutinizes small corporations closely. Unlike a sole proprietorship or a partnership, forming a corporation requires the sale of shares in company stock, and regular meetings of the board of directors must be documented. Under a corporate structure, you would have to live with a fixed salary, whereas a sole proprietorship allows unrestricted access to company funds. Also, naming your corporation after yourself is an IRS red flag, since it could be perceived as a proprietorship posing as a corporation.

Advantages

- Protection of personal assets
- Transfer of shares to investors or stockholders
- Ease of raising capital
- Ability to separate business functions into different corporations

Disadvantages

- Increased legal and operational formalities
- Power limited by charter
- Less freedom of activity
- Decreased control by owner

If you're incorporating and want to purchase a corporate kit (stock certificates, seal, and bylaws) without going through a lawyer, contact:

Corpex Bank Note Company, Inc.
1440 Fifth Avenue
Bayshore, NY 11706
(800) 221-8181

Your Office Equipment and the Computer Age

Although you can run your business without a computer, having one certainly affords a distinct advantage. A PC will save you hours in record keeping, maintaining mailing lists,

POWERTIP

For free, expert advice on running your business, consider the Service Corps of Retired Executives (SCORE). Check the Blue Pages of your telephone directory for the SCORE office near you, or write to:

National SCORE Office
Small Business Administration
409 Third Street, Suite 500
Washington, D.C. 20416

personalizing sales letters, processing orders, and desktop publishing. Business service centers such as Kinko's rent computers by the hour, and they can even teach you how to use the computer for an additional charge.

Even if you're starting out on a shoestring budget, eventually you will be able to afford your own equipment, which can lower costs and increase efficiency. You can outfit your office with basic equipment for between $2,500 and $4,000 (tax-deductible expenses, of course). Don't run out and buy everything all at once; wait until your business is making a profit and you really need the equipment. And remember, prices changes extremely quickly, so watch the sales and forgive me if my numbers here are slightly off. Here are some of the basics that you should eventually have:

PERSONAL COMPUTER

There are two categories of personal computer: IBM and Apple Macintosh. A basic IBM computer that uses DOS (Disc Operating System), including a 486 microprocessor, four or eight megabytes of RAM (random access memory), and a 200-plus megabyte hard drive, should cost about $1,400. The Apple Macintosh PowerMac includes a PowerPC microprocessor, comes with eight megabytes of RAM, and costs from $1,600 to $5,000, depending on speed and hard drive capacity.

MULTIMEDIA PERSONAL COMPUTER

These deluxe personal computers include a CD-ROM drive, color monitor, sound capabilities, and built-in fax modem. It is essential that you at least have a fax modem to access the Internet and to send and receive faxes, two fundamentals of modern home businesses. Depending on speed, size of memory, and monitor quality/size, prices start at $1,600.

SOFTWARE

There is a variety of software on the market for every part of your business, from word processing, desktop publishing, and record keeping, to filing and spreadsheets. Assess your needs and shop around for the best deals. I like Microsoft Word for word processing and Adobe PageMaker for desktop publishing; both are easy-to-use, quality products.

PRINTER

There are three types of printers for your computer. The dot matrix printer is the cheapest (about $100), but the resolution is poor. Ink-jet printers (about $250) are essential for letter-quality output and require pricey replacement ink cartridges (about $30 each). The best (and most expensive) is a laser printer, which provides print-shop-quality results. Laser printers are available in black-and-white or color, and cost between $500 and $2,000 or more.

FAX MACHINE

If you don't have a multimedia computer with a built-in fax modem, you may want to buy a fax machine. You can get a basic model for about $200. Choose a fax machine that prints on regular paper to avoid the frustration of curling, heat-sensitive fax paper.

DESKTOP COPIER

Cheaper models cost about $400, but are slow and don't include automatic paper feed. For large jobs, faster models with automatic paper feed cost about $1,000. A cheaper alternative is to lease. Check the Yellow Pages under "Copiers."

TELEPHONE/ANSWERING MACHINE

Both are relatively inexpensive, but you'll need at least two lines or call waiting in order to conduct business in a professional

POWERTIP

The Independent Business Alliance offers group medical and business insurance, merchant status, loans, legal and accounting services, telecommunications (including 800 numbers), and discounted office supplies and services. A one-year membership costs forty-nine dollars. For information, call (800) 450-2422.

manner. When getting a new business phone, ask for a number that translates into letters that relate to your business. Before you call the phone company, make a list of several possibilities and ask if they are available. There's no extra charge, and you'll gain a lot of marketing mileage as a result.

Ten Tips for a Productive Home Office

Back in school, there was a big difference between work done in the classroom and "homework." The same is true for a home-based business. Working at home demands plenty of self-discipline. Fortunately, unlike the boredom of schoolwork, with a home business you are doing something you love—not to mention putting food on the dinner table. Nonetheless, working at home poses unique challenges that need to be addressed.

Here are some helpful tips:

1. Set up your office in the quietest, most remote area of the house, away from noise and regular household disruptions.
2. Keep your home life and business life separate. This means separating phone lines for personal and business use, keeping personal and business records in separate files, and using separate credit cards for business expenses.
3. Make sure the family understands and respects the fact that when you're in the office you're at work and must not be disturbed for trivial reasons. Nothing is more unprofessional than a wailing child or a barking dog in the background during a business call. The fact that you work at home doesn't mean that you don't need child care, unless your kids are in school all day.
4. Keep your office supplies in the office. Buy separate supplies for family use, so you'll always know where to find your scissors, tape, or paper clips when you need them.

5. Rent a post office box near your home to receive business mail. This will keep your mail from getting mixed up with personal mail.

6. Manage your time wisely. When you were an employee, you could get away with a four-martini lunch or gossip with coworkers around the water cooler and still get paid. In a home-based business, productivity is paramount, and the expression "time is money" takes on renewed importance. Focus and prioritize. Compile a "to do" list, and schedule the most important tasks for the time of day when you're at your best.

7. Make time each day to read. Catch up on the latest industry trade magazines, newsletters, and mailers. Save what you need in a "reference" file for future review, separate from your "current" file. Set aside at least one day a week to make phone calls and catch up on paperwork. Group similar tasks such as paperwork, phone calls, and errands together.

8. Keep business contacts organized, and make sure the information is current. If you're the disorganized sort (like me), who accumulates information on bits of paper scattered all over the office, be sure to put them in order before you quit for the day, while they're still fresh in your mind. Better yet, invest in a small hand-held tape recorder, and dictate your messages for later transcription.

9. Clean up at the end of each day. Walking into a disaster area isn't the most inspiring way to begin the day. I try to wrap up each day with a tidy desk and a fresh "to do" list for the next day, so that if I arrive a little groggy the next morning, at least I know where I left off. This allows me to tackle something simple while I'm waking up.

10. Don't forget an exercise routine. Don't become a slave to the office. Get out to the gym for a workout at least three times a week, to keep your mind sharp and your energy level high.

When designing your home office, practicality, efficiency, and safety are prime concerns. Two helpful booklets on the subject are *Lighting in the Healthy Office*, (800) 777-0330, and *The Ergonomics and Office Design Workbook*, (800) 344-2600. (See the Resource Directory for more details.)

POWERTIP

When considering home-office and business equipment insurance, call the Insurance Information Institute's consumer hot line, at (212) 669-9200. The hot line is one of the best, and can provide you with a comprehensive, affordable policy to protect your investment.

PART TWO

Dynamarketing Strategies

CHAPTER 3

MAIL-ORDER MASTERY: IF MONEY GREW ON TREES, THIS WOULD BE THE ORCHARD

*Difficulties mastered are
opportunities won.*

Winston Churchill

MARKETING IS THE PROCESS of getting your product or idea to the consumer. You need to know what the consumer wants and how to communicate your message in a way that compels them to buy. If you offer a quality product that will enhance people's lives at a fair price, remove the consumer's risk with a convenient money-back guarantee, and toss in a free bonus, you will prosper. Stick to this basic formula, and you'll never need to resort to smoke and mirrors.

We are bombarded with an average of 1,500 advertising messages every day. Even the sanctity of a public washroom stall has become fair game. When you combine this saturation with increasing consumer resistance and expectations, it becomes clear that the big winners of the future will be advertisers who under-promise and over-deliver. This includes:

- Quality and value
- Convenience and service
- Unconditional, hassle-free warranties

Target Your Market

Despite the popular saying, it doesn't necessarily take money to make money. It does, however, require a strong game plan, along with a generous helping of resources and inspiration. This means finding and focusing on your *target market.* People routinely fail because they fire all their ammunition trying to hit anything and everything. It doesn't take long before they run out of ammo. Aim for the bull's-eye. It's unrealistic to go after 100 percent of the market. Even the most successful product has competition. The key is to go after your piece of the action, or *market share.*

Pick Your Product or Service Wisely

Improve on an existing product by making it better, cheaper, or more convenient. Keep up with the latest fads and trends. Read magazines and newspapers and watch TV. News magazine shows like *60 Minutes, Dateline NBC, 20/20,* and even prime-time dramas and sitcoms are a reflection of what's hot in America.

Go to the records section of the library and browse through old patents. You'll find them on microfiche or computer disk. This is a superb source of ideas similar to yours, as well as forgotten ideas that may be revived with the right twist or upgrade. Trade journals related to your field are also a valuable source of people, products, and ideas that can help you.

If you're looking for existing products to sell, contact the mail-order wholesalers listed in the Resource Directory for information and a free catalog.

How to Do Your Own Market Research

Modern technology has made it possible to test almost any idea you have. It's no longer necessary to spend hundreds of thousands of dollars on market research. In fact, common sense will take you a surprisingly long way toward understanding the fundamentals of dynamarketing. The number one rule is: know what your potential customers are thinking!

MARKET RESEARCH FUNDAMENTALS

1. Identify the target customers for your product or service.
2. Find out all you can about your target customers' habits, needs, preferences, and buying cycles. Your local chamber of commerce can point you to a wealth of sources.
3. Determine the most cost-effective, efficient way to reach your target customers in order to generate sales, be it direct mail, trade magazine advertisements, etc.

INFORMATION SOURCES

You can get all the feedback you need from three basic sources:

- Family and friends
- Coworkers and other people you know
- Experts and suppliers in the field of your endeavor

Experts and suppliers might even become strategic partners in your planning, production, or marketing. You don't have to pay these people for their expertise; it can be obtained through telephone calls and queries. If you later decide to bring strategic partners aboard, always offer to pay them out of the net, not the gross. This is what's left after you've covered your overhead.

Start by asking questions, and follow the thread until you acquire the information and contacts you need. A few questions to ask:

- Do they like your idea? If so, why? If not, why?
- What changes do they suggest?
- What price would they be willing to pay for it?
- Who and where do they think the customers are?

POWERTIP

The National Marketing Federation will answer your questions about marketing and sources by telephone for a small fee. Call (800) 2-SOLVE-IT. They also review questions via fax at no cost.

- How would they reach these customers?
- Who do they know who could be of further help to you?

Don't be fooled by what you *want* to hear as opposed to what you *need* to hear. Press for the truth; it's the only way to acquire the information you need. Likewise, don't look to retail buyers for approval. They're accustomed to patronizing people because they know most ideas never get past the dream stage anyway. If a retail buyer tells you how wonderful your product is, cut to the chase by asking, "So, how many units would you like to order?"

One of the more popular marketing strategies involves comparing one product to another, head-to-head. Pepsi compares itself to Coke, Burger King to McDonald's, etc. This method is called "benchmarking." Unfortunately, benchmarking backfires more often than it works, because most people tend to perceive the first product that comes to mind as superior. The key to successful dynamarketing lies in *perceptions* as opposed to products. Neil Armstrong was the first human to walk on the moon. Who was the second? Henry Ford built the first automobile. Who built the second?

People are more interested in what's new than what's better. Why waste time and money comparing your widget to the competition, when there's a more forceful way to position yourself in the market? When developing a new product or idea, the first question you should ask yourself is, "If I can't be the first in an existing category, what new category can I create that I can be first in?" Find that category and promote it aggressively. Target the widest possible market, concentrating on mass appeal. Remember, it's usually better to sell water than wine, since everybody drinks water.

As the saying goes, first impressions are everything, and perception is reality. It's true, people don't like to change their minds. Can you recall the last time you made a less-than-favorable impression on someone that the person clung to, despite all your efforts to change his or her mind? Dynamarketing works the same way. The only way to change one person's perception of reality is to change the same perception in other people's minds, until the majority outnumbers the minority. An individual who feels out of touch with the majority is more likely to change his or her mind. Although you may be unable to change a person's mind, the majority can. This is the secret of influencing both perception and reality . . . very powerful stuff!

Avoid the temptation to rush your product to market. This is where fatal mistakes are made. No matter how excited you are or how much adulation you receive, keep a level head until your marketing network is established. Never risk your money on an untested idea. Always wait until your income supports the risk.

Value-for-Value Dynamarketing Summary

- Fill an unmet need. Identify a problem and provide a solution.
- Improve on an existing product or service. Create a category in which you can be first.
- Emphasize benefits over features.
- Be honest. In business, integrity is everything.
- Discount the retail price. Show the customer what an outstanding deal they're getting.
- Include a bonus. Everyone appreciates a terrific deal.
- If it makes a great gift, say so.
- Unconditionally guarantee customer satisfaction. Remove the resistance by eliminating the risk.

Product Pricing

Whether you purchase products wholesale to resell, or have your product manufactured from scratch (books, audiotapes, etc.), the following information will help you arrive

POWERTIP

Check out *Guerrilla Marketing for Home-Based Business* by consultant Jay Conrad Levinson (see the Resource Directory). Levinson also offers a free weekly newsletter on inexpensive marketing strategies, in addition to a selection of downloadable tips on his Web site at *http:// www.gmarketing.com*.

at the right price to cover your costs, shipping, and overhead while ensuring sufficient profit to keep your business in the black.

1. **Direct Material Costs:** Calculate the cost of materials required to manufacture your product, based on quotes from manufacturers, printers, etc. Total the cost of an initial "run" of your product, then divide by the number of units to arrive at your cost per unit. Remember to factor in discounts for volume and quantity. The larger the run, the bigger the discount.

2. **Direct Labor Costs:** Calculate the cost of any outside labor involved in producing your product. Divide that figure by the number of units, and add it to the Direct Material Costs total:

   Materials + Labor = $_____

3. **Overhead Expenses:** These include advertising, packing materials, shipping, office supplies, postage, taxes, repairs, maintenance, etc. In order to be as accurate as possible, calculate logical, even slightly inflated figures for all your expenses. If you work at home, include a portion of your total rent or mortgage payment (in proportion to your work space and storage areas). List all overhead expenses by month and total them, then divide the total overhead by the number of units per run:

   Overhead + Materials + Labor = Total Cost per Unit

4. **Profit:** Factor your profit margin into the cost of each unit to avoid merely breaking even—one of the most common reasons for business failure. Study your competition to see what they're charging. If your product is superior to the competition, charge a little more. If your product is comparable, price it similarly. Be sure to set your profit margin before you factor the competition. Remember, the main purpose of a business is to make a profit. Finally, add the profit margin to the total cost per unit to arrive at your total price per unit.

Your cost of materials should be no more than 25 percent of your retail price. If your product costs twenty dollars to make, it should retail for about eighty dollars. This gives you the best chance of selling your product slightly above your total cost (after advertising) and show a profit, or at least break even.

Compare existing products with your own. Study the competition in trade magazines to see how they're doing at the price they charge. While a higher price can mean lower sales, consumers are also impressed with and remember a quality upscale item, which can lead to repeat sales and upsell opportunities (the sale of additional products or upgrades to existing customers). Order everything on the market that resembles your product. If necessary, you can always return it for a refund after you've examined it. This guerrilla market research enables you to separate the bona fide from the bogus, build a better mousetrap, and avoid introducing a product that is already meeting consumer demand.

PRICE POINTS

Price points are the psychological buttons your offer will push in the consumer's mind in terms of perceived cost versus benefits. Think of price points in terms of "tens." For example, $9.95 is more desirable than $11.95, since $11.95 exceeds the ten-dollar price point. Whenever a price point is surpassed, you encounter an increased level of buyer resistance.

You can make price points work to your advantage by adding a surcharge for shipping and handling (S&H). Instead of charging $22.95 for your product, you can remain below the twenty-dollar price point by changing the offer to $19.95 plus $3.00 S&H. The total is still $22.95, however you're still below the $20.00 price point in the customer's mind. Although this may seem to be splitting hairs, the result can be a substantial increase in response rate. Similarly, $19.95 is better than $19.99. Why? Your guess is as good as mine. Just call it an "industry standard."

Advertising Your Product

Time for a lesson in basic copywriting. You don't need to be a genius in order to write engaging copy. Take it from someone who wrote radio commercials for 15 years. When you are passionate and believe in your product, it's easy to talk about it. I'm merely going to provide the basic fundamentals (and a few tricks of the trade) that will put a little "sizzle into the steak."

How to Write Winning Ads

Draw attention to your ad by leading with powerful, eye-catching words like these:

> MIRACLE
> INCREDIBLE
> NEW
> HOW TO
> IMPORTANT
> FREE
> YOU
> IMPROVED
> AMAZING

Keeping your ad brief and to the point will keep your costs down, allowing you to run more ads in a variety of publications and extend your reach. Make the strongest possible statement about your service. Write the kind of ad you would respond to. Show rough drafts to friends and family and get their unbiased reactions.

"Makes a Great Gift!"

How many times have you heard this phrase? It's very effective. Whether we live in New York or North Platte, we love to buy for others. Christmas, birthdays, weddings, showers, Mother's Day, Father's Day . . . gifts are big business. If your product or idea makes a great gift, don't be shy about saying so.

Golden Rules of Advertising

- Command attention.
- Keep it short and simple.
- Emphasize benefits over features.

The term "benefits over features" simply means emphasizing the direct benefits the reader will receive from your product, as opposed to listing the features or details. Features have their place, but benefits are more powerful. For example:

> Features: *This sports car has jet-black paint and high-performance radial tires.*
> Benefits: *This car will take you from zero to sixty in 8.5 seconds and make you feel like a million bucks!*

Notice the difference? Write from the reader's perspective, focusing on what they will feel as they read your ad and how they'll positively benefit from your product. The tried-and-true formula for winning ads is:

Grab the reader's or listener's attention with a killer headline or lead statement. Ask a question that addresses a problem or unmet need. Truthfully and convincingly tell your story, and establish rapport in an appealing, informative style. Write as you speak, using all your powers of persuasion. Remember these advertising basics:

> USP: Unique Selling Position
> AIDA: Attention → Interest → Desire → Action
> FAB: Fact → Advantage → Benefit

Pick up any magazine and study the ads. Borrow an idea here and a catch phrase there until you've created an absolutely killer ad.

THE "HOT BUTTON"

The hot button is the issue that your prospect is most concerned about. The better you are at locating and addressing this need, the more successful you'll be. You find the hot button by asking questions such as "What is your biggest concern?" and "What do you expect most from this product?" You've got to know what your audience wants. Make

---

POWERTIP

The Corporate Design Foundation is a nonprofit group that publishes a free quarterly newsletter called @*issue* for small-business owners. Fax a subscription request to (617) 451-6355.

them believe in you and your product. Learn from your mistakes. Great copywriting is an ongoing process.

USING AN ADVERTISING AGENCY

While virtually everything you need to plan and execute a successful marketing campaign is included in this book, sometimes an ad agency can provide valuable expertise and get you volume discounts on multimedia buys. As you move from classified ads to display ads, a good agency can help you with everything from ad design, copywriting, and production, to making buys in the best media to reach your customers. Usually, agencies take a 15 percent commission of your advertising expenditures. Finding an agency is as easy as checking the Yellow Pages, or you can peruse ads in magazines, making a list of the ads that run consistently. Call the advertisers and ask for the name of their agency, then call the agency and explain your needs.

The agency doesn't have to be in your home town, although cross-town may be cheaper than cross-country. A reputable agency will provide you with both advice and an honest estimate to meet your requirements. Be sure to include all your specifications and a sample of your ad if possible. List your price points, and include copies of existing ads that mirror your own. While an agency that specializes in a particular medium (radio, print, etc.) will naturally try to steer you in that direction, you always have the final call. Be suspicious of any agency that:

- doesn't provide comprehensive research when you ask for it.
- pressures you into buying a load of ads before testing the market.
- is unwilling to prove itself by working with you on a test basis.

You hire an advertising agency for one reason only: results. A good agency will ask questions about your product. Give them as much information as possible. This will help them develop a research proposal that doesn't cost you anything unless you decide to go with it. Ask for a month's worth of free ads. If they work, you can move up to a larger test. Move cautiously. This will weed out cookie-cutter operations that are only in it for the quick sale.

SAVE MONEY WITH AN IN-HOUSE AD AGENCY

Set up your own "in-house" ad agency. Agencies can often obtain discounted advertising space for their customers, so if you write your own ad copy, this is the way to go. You simply establish an in-house agency, then represent yourself. Many businesses and corporations have their own in-house agencies. However, it must be a separate entity from your primary business, and you must register the name with the county clerk's office. Design separate letterhead, envelopes, and insertion order forms. Just fill out the form and enclose your ad copy and payment, less a 15 percent agency discount and a 2 percent cash discount if applicable, and send it to the magazine or newspaper.

Unfortunately, the existence of unprofessional, mom-and-pop in-house agencies has resulted in tighter restrictions on discounts allowed by some of the major media. They won't recognize your in-house agency unless they believe you are legitimate. Make sure your letterhead and insertion order forms are professional looking. Brush up on advertising terminology so you can talk the talk. Start by approaching smaller publications, and it won't be long before you learn the ropes.

GETTING THE MOST FOR YOUR ADVERTISING DOLLAR

July and December are the slowest months for direct response. When buying advertising of any kind, always negotiate as many extras you can. This includes free mentions in the New Products or What's New section, interviews, and guest articles. If buying radio or TV ad time, ask for "spins"—bonus commercials, in addition to your paid schedule, that run in late night or unsold air time. Remember, you're in charge. Always try to get as much as you possibly can for your advertising dollar.

Remnant Ads: How to Get 50 Percent or More off the Rate Card

Just as radio and television stations have perishable inventory that goes to waste if unsold, so do newspapers and magazines. You can get discounts of 50 percent or more by going after remnant, or unsold, print ad space.

Here's how it works. Let's say you're the publisher of a small magazine. Upon receiving the layout of next month's issue, you discover you have two or three blank pages staring you in the face. What do you do? You could add another article, a subscription offer, or maybe even a public service announcement—none of which will bring in the revenue of a paid ad. But wait! You just remembered that package you received from the person who sent you a camera-ready ad, along with a letter certifying that she would pay a certain amount for a remnant ad. You insert the ad into one of the extra pages, and send the advertiser an invoice for the amount specified.

Remnant agreements are usually made ahead of time, in the form of a letter signed by you and the publisher. Start by making a few calls. You could be turned down several times before finding an open door. It can be worth it, believe me. Determine what you're willing to pay, learn each publication's policies and deadlines, then send the necessary paperwork along with a camera-ready ad. Being "politely persistent" (not a pain in the neck) can get you a premium-space ad for peanuts!

"Keying" Your Ads

If you're running a lot of ads in a number of publications, you'll need a system to keep track of where the orders are coming from in order to determine which ads are performing and which are not. There are a number of different ways to do this. Here is one of the more common keying systems:

FS-03/7

"FS" refers to the publication in which your ad appeared (e.g., *Field & Stream*).
"03" is the month of issue (March).
"7" refers to the year (1997).

> **POWERTIP**
>
> When advertising in newspapers, always use the television listing page or pullout section. The premium is worth it, since tests have shown response rates to be ten-to-one over ads in any other section.

If you are testing your ads for different price points, you can add an "A" to the key code for one price, and a "B" for the second, in order to track which ad generates the most sales. Choose the system that works best for you.

ESTIMATING RESPONSE

Here is a system for determine the total response, or "pull," generated by your ads. Tally the number of orders from the first day they start coming in until the corresponding date according to publication (see Table 3.1). Double that figure to estimate your total pull.

The heaviest mail days are usually Monday and Friday. Tuesday is the lightest. One pound of mail is equal to roughly 100 envelopes. When the orders come pouring in, it might be more efficient to weigh your mail than to count it.

Maintain a list of your customers' names and addresses. You may want to sell to them again, or rent the names to mailing-list companies for an additional source of revenue.

Mail-Order Mastery

Mail order is one of the most exciting and profitable home business opportunities available. The playing field is wide open, with limitless opportunity. You don't need a special

TABLE 3.1
Estimating Response to an Advertisement

TYPE OF AD	TOTAL PULL	FORMULA
Direct Mailings	Orders × 30	Days × 2
Daily Publications	Orders × 30	Days × 2
Weekly Publications	Orders × 10	Days × 2
Monthly Publications	Orders × 20	Days × 2
Bimonthly Publications	Orders × 30	Days × 2

▌ **POWERTIP**

▌ For a free brochure on how to use leaflets and bulletin boards for
▌ advertising, call Thumbtack Bugle at (510) 653-8063.

education, the required start-up capital is minimal, and
there's a market for anything you can think of. Even with
the emergence of infomercials and home shopping, mail
order continues to thrive. It has been estimated that by the
end of the decade, annual revenue from catalog sales alone
will exceed $75 billion.

Lillian Vernon was a housewife who enjoyed making personalized leather purses at her kitchen table and selling them
by mail. In 1994, the now-famous Lillian Vernon Catalog
grossed more than $155 million! Mail order is here to stay.

Whether you choose to sell your own products or purchase from one of the many mail-order wholesalers, the key
is to find something that motivates and excites you, and communicate that passion to consumers.

DIRECT-MAIL ADVERTISING

Direct marketing by mail is one of the best ways to reach potential customers. Direct mail targets customers with a
personal approach, one on one, and allows you to enclose
more information about your product than you can in a classified or even a display ad. Direct mail also makes it tougher
for your competitors to eavesdrop on your operation.
Simmons Market Research Bureau reports that 67 percent of
consumers open direct mail, 30 percent open some and throw
the rest away, and 3 percent throw it all away.

There is a horde of scam artists operating by direct mail,
which has led to increased consumer resistance. Be prepared
to address these concerns in your sales literature if this is a
problem in your field. Since a cheap-looking mailer is the
first sign of a potential rip-off, your package must be completely honest and professional. You don't have to spend a
lot of money on expensive paper or elaborate graphics. Inexpensive alternatives include photographs, clip art, and
colored paper.

A high-impact direct-mail package should include the following elements:

1. **The sales letter:** This is the most crucial element of your mailer, since it creates the first impression and subsequent rapport between you and the reader. While similar to a display ad in content, it should be more like a personal letter, and include a headline, byline, and anywhere from two to six pages of copy that explain the benefits and features of your product in detail. Remember, the headline is 90 percent of your presentation; it has to grab the reader's attention. The most successful letters usually average about four pages. Of course, the more expensive the product, the more space you'll need to sell it.

   Draw attention to crucial words and phrases by using CAPS, **bold type**, *italics*, and underlining. Don't go overboard. Unjustified (open) right margins are preferable to justified (even) margins (the text in this book uses justified margins). Tests have shown unjustified margins to be more appealing to the reader.

   Including a photograph adds attractiveness to your letter. A "P.S." at the end draws attention, and gives you the chance to repeat a key benefit or bonus. Don't forget to include your return address in the letter. If a customer loses the order form, you'll still get the sale.

2. **The brochure:** This is where you create even more interest by stating the dominant selling points of your offer in a concise, easy-to-read format. Include a photograph or illustration printed on glossy or colored paper.

3. **The order form:** This can either be a separate coupon or part of the sales letter or brochure. Check out a few magazine or direct-mail ads to get a feel for the format. A detachable money-back guarantee provides reinforcement and makes it easy for your customer to keep track of his or her order. Since mailing lists contain approximately 10 percent errors in names or addresses, don't attach the address label to the order form; let your customers fill in the correct information on the coupon. If you have an 800 number for credit card ordering, be sure to display it prominently.

4. **The mailing envelope:** The right envelope is important, since the first step is to get someone to open it. Don't clutter the envelope; anything more than the mailing address and return address identifies your package as junk mail in

the minds of many people. Some copywriters use a catchy question or phrase like: *"Of course you can win the lottery! Let me show you how!"* I prefer a clean, unobtrusive look. Test a few variations to find out what works best for you. Use a number ten window envelope, and attach the address label to the back of the circular, letter, or order form so that it shows through. Provide only your return address—no company name. This adds an element of intrigue. The more official-looking the envelope, the more compelled the recipient will be to open it. I like the subtle approach.

5. **The return envelope:** This is the smaller (number six or eight), self-addressed envelope your customer will use to mail in the order form. Although reply envelopes might seem to be an unnecessary expense, they easily pay for themselves in increased response.

6. **Testimonials:** Endorsements from satisfied customers do a lot for your credibility. Keep a record of positive comments until you have enough to put together a decent list. You'll have to obtain written permission from the writer in order to print them. One more thing: "Lynn Smith, Lakewood, FL" is more believable than "L.S., Lakewood FL."

MAILING LISTS

A good list is the single most important factor in your success with direct mail. The three kinds of mailing lists are compiled lists, direct-response lists, and your own "in-house" customer list.

Compiled lists contain names and addresses that have been gathered according to demographic or occupational similarity. These are discount lists that are advertised for "$50 for 10,000 names," and are considered to be inferior mail-response lists.

Direct-response lists are comprised of people who have previously purchased products by mail, and are the best lists for targeting consumers who are interested in products like yours. Direct-response lists are further narrowed into "buyer" lists (those who actually purchased) and "inquiry" lists (those who responded for free details from an ad, but didn't necessarily purchase the products). A buyer list is always better than an inquiry list.

The only list you have free use of is your own list. You must rent the others from a mailing list company on a one-time-only basis. It is illegal to copy or use a rented list twice. Lists are "seeded" with random decoy names to prevent unauthorized use. If you use a list more than once, your mailer will arrive at the decoy address a second time, and you could be sued. However, you can use your own list as often as you like, and even rent it to dozens of list companies on a profit-per-use basis.

Finding the Right Mailing List This can be an intimidating task for the beginner. There are literally tens of thousands of list companies. The best way to find a good list is through a list broker or manager. These people specialize in locating the best list for your offer. Since brokers and managers are paid by list companies, you don't pay directly for their services. For a directory of list companies, managers, and brokers, look to the Standard Rate and Data Service's *Direct Mail List Rates & Data,* listed in the Resource Directory.

The Golden Rule with mailing lists is, "you get what you pay for." Avoid cheap lists; always use "hot" lists. These include the names of people who have purchased products in the most recent quarter, or ninety-day period. The going rate for a good list ranges between sixty and ninety dollars per thousand names. Send a copy of your direct-mail package to the broker or manager to help them find the most effective list for your campaign. Find out where the list originated, and get a copy of the ad that generated the names on the list. You can also ask for the names of other direct marketers who have used the list to find out how they did.

A certain amount of undeliverable mail, or "nixies," is inevitable. Minimize this by choosing a list company that guarantees 95 to 98 percent deliverability, or offers credit toward future lists.

PRESORT SERVICES

When you receive your direct-mail materials from the printer, you'll need a presort service to sort, fold, and stuff the materials into envelopes, apply address labels and postage, and mail the finished product. They can even add a bar code to your return envelopes for speedy delivery; the post office uses automation to process bar-coded mail. Look for presort companies in the Yellow Pages under "Mailing Services," and shop around for the best deal.

POSTAGE

Go First Class instead of Bulk Rate. Not only does First Class mail have a higher deliverability ratio than bulk mail, but your orders will arrive sooner, since they'll reach your customers faster. Try to avoid printed postage permits. A thirty-two-cent stamp or a metered postage stamp increases response because they're more personal.

Avoid doing a direct-mail campaign during the Christmas and Thanksgiving holidays. These are the worst response periods for selling information or anything other than holiday gifts. Near Christmas, time your mailer to arrive no earlier than the first week of January. At Thanksgiving, time your campaign to pull at least 70 percent of the response prior to the holiday.

POSTCARDS

Postcards are an inexpensive and effective way to conduct a direct-mail campaign. You not only avoid the monotony of folding and stuffing envelopes yourself and the expense of hiring a presort company, but postcards only cost twenty cents each to mail. While response rates for postcards may be slightly lower than for complete direct-mail packages, they are still an effective and less expensive method for getting a customer to contact you for more details.

The headline must command immediate attention and interest since postcards are usually the first items to be thrown away as people sort their mail. Print size is slightly smaller than average; ten-point type as opposed to twelve. Rely heavily on benefits and features. Use a limited-time offer, and include a discounted price and/or free bonus for prompt response (seven to ten days). Don't forget the money-back guarantee.

For discount rates on postcard printing (about four cents each) contact:

Henry Birtle and Sons
1143 East Colorado Street
Glendale, CA 91205
(818) 241-1598

CARD DECKS

You can either mail card decks to your own list, or cooperate with other advertisers (see the list of co-op mailing companies in the Resource Directory). This is cheaper than doing your own mailer, however, your message may get lost in the crowd. It is best to use as a secondary option. The Standard Rate and Data Service lists more than 600 card decks in its *Business Publication Rates and Data Directory*, available in the reference section of your library.

TEST, TEST, TEST

The best method for testing your direct-mail campaign is to buy a hot list of 5,000 names, minimum. You'll need at least that many to get an accurate response. To do a test from a list of more than 5,000 names, simply remove every third, fifth, or tenth name, until the list is pared down to 5,000. This will give you a random geographic mix of names. Test the hot list before ordering older lists, and test those, too. Rushing blindly into a direct-mail campaign is a recipe for financial disaster. Also test your mailer, substituting different headlines and copy points to see what works best before you get into an extensive campaign. You can keep track of your tests using standard key codes.

Order Fulfillment

This is where things begin to get exciting! At last, the orders are showing up in your mail box. Now you have the cash to cover your initial expenses and your printing and shipping costs. Best of all, you're finally making a profit. Fulfill orders as soon as possible. Deposit checks and money orders into your account, and get the necessary run of inventory. This can take anywhere from one to five weeks, depending on the size of your order and the manufacturer's turnaround time. Make sure you're aware of this in advance.

Purchase envelopes and address labels in bulk. Ask about bulk mail rates at the post office, or use the services of a fulfillment company or mail-order house (check the Yellow Pages). They will package and ship your product. Rates are reasonable, and you'll save hours of work.

Sales Tax

A 1992 U.S. Supreme Court ruling determined that states cannot force mail-order companies to collect sales tax from consumers, but there is a possibility that Congress may reverse that decision. Today sales tax does not apply to out-of-state transactions, but it is imposed on purchases made within the taxing state. If the transaction is for a service, state sales taxes generally do not apply. If your sales occur outside your home state, it's your responsibility to keep appropriate records (postal receipts and customer lists) as proof of out-of-state delivery.

Municipal sales taxes do not apply unless the transaction occurs within the taxing municipality. Legally, the place of sale is the location where the buyer takes possession of merchandise. Use taxes may apply to purchases that are not subject to state sales tax in the originating state. Liability for use tax belongs to the consumer and not the seller.

There are many organizations and publications listed in the Resource Directory that can answer your questions regarding tax obligations. The IRS offers a helpful service designed to guide small-business operators through the process of record keeping and tax forms called the Small Business Tax Education Program (STEP). Contact your local IRS office for details.

CHAPTER 4

NEWSPAPER CLASSIFIEDS: SPECTACULAR SAVINGS AND POWER PROFITS

Often the difference between a successful person and a failure is not in abilities or ideas, but in the courage to bet on ideas, take calculated risks—and act.

Maxwell Maltz

HERE'S SOME HIGH-POWERED INFORMATION that will save you a great deal of time and money while generating thousands of inquiries for your product or service. The American Publishing Company and independent state press associations nationwide will place ads for you in hundreds of newspapers at a time. The process is ridiculously easy: you place one order that gets your classified ad in newspapers statewide or nationwide. It's a convenient, highly effective classified advertising system that allows you to reach millions of readers across the country with a single phone call.

To place your ad in 1,000 newspapers the old way, you'd spend $320 on postage stamps alone, not to mention expensive long-distance bills. Entrepreneurs who place ads are earning upwards of $10,000 a day with this amazing system. Now you can use it to place classified advertisements for 900 numbers, publications, or products and services. You could even start a business as a classified ad "broker," and earn substantial commissions placing ads for other people. A Texas couple recently grossed a million dollars just from placing ads for businesses that had no idea this incredible resource existed!

American Publishing Company

American Publishing Company (APC) owns more than 300 newspapers and supplements in twenty-nine states, with a combined readership of more than three million people. APC targets active mail-order buyers in the heartland of America—the rural market. One call gets your classified ad in one state, a combination of states, or all twenty-nine available states. This saves hours of time and expense placing ads the old way, one by one.

A twenty-five word ad that runs in all 300 papers for one day costs only about $330 ($1.10 per ad, with a $7 charge for additional words). This is their nationwide Plan A. Supplemental discounts are available for multi-week orders. They also offer a statewide plan, including papers covering forty-six states with a total circulation of forty million subscribers (Plan B, see Table 4.1). APC can also place your classifieds in specific metropolitan areas (Plan C, see Table 4.2).

The APC Canadian Network includes nine dailies and sixteen weeklies, with a combined circulation of 440,500. Rates are $170 for fifteen words, and $8.75 for each additional word.

See the following rate schedule (subject to change). Contact APC for current rates and a customized reach plan to meet your needs. For information:

American Publishing Company
P.O. Box 7
Macon, MO 64552
(800) 475-3121
Fax: (816) 385-3082

TABLE 4.1
American Publishing Company—Statewide Plan B

STATE	RATE/ 25 WORDS	EXTRA WORDS	TOTAL PUBLICATIONS	CIRCULATION
Alabama	$202.50	$8.10	106	880,000
Arizona	174.15	6.75	61	550,000
Arkansas	174.15	6.75	106	954,384
California	460.00	17.25	186	3,300,000
Colorado	202.50	6.75	99	558,000
Florida	287.50	5.75	83	1,155,100
Georgia	230.00	6.90	103	1,200,000
Idaho	148.50	6.75	48	310,000
Illinois	345.00	6.90	182	900,000
Indiana	172.50	5.75	90	900,000
Iowa	222.75	9.45	244	1,322,700
Kansas	148.50	8.10	85	420,300
Kentucky	171.35	6.76	70	1,200,000
Louisiana	168.75	8.10	83	540,500
Maryland	172.50	6.90	67	1,300,000
Michigan	345.00	6.90	117	1,500,000
Minnesota	201.15	8.10	275	1,800,000
Mississippi	143.75	6.90	90	620,000
Missouri	149.00	6.00	165	907,000
Montana	133.65	5.40	59	208,000
Nebraska	155.25	6.75	185	500,000
Nevada	113.85	5.75	25	440,000
New England*	270.25	5.75	188	2,029,000
New Jersey	295.65	12.15	94	1,200,000
New Mexico	121.50	6.75	27	222,230
New York	276.00	10.35	241	1,597,000
North Carolina	230.00	6.90	102	1,447,000
North Dakota	133.65	6.75	92	350,000
Ohio	175.50	8.10	104	1,000,000
Oklahoma	201.25	9.20	169	1,500,000
Oregon	270.00	10.80	62	539,400
Pennsylvania	337.50	13.50	158	2,400,000
South Carolina	230.00	6.90	72	763,000
South Dakota	155.25	5.75	148	385,000
Tennessee	133.65	5.40	61	400,000
Texas	337.50	13.50	301	1,800,000
Utah	113.85	3.45	42	380,000
Virginia	236.25	8.10	62	1,819,800
Washington	174.15	5.40	94	1,000,000
West Virginia	168.75	6.75	56	709,300
Wisconsin	159.85	4.60	200	1,605,000
Wyoming	147.15	6.75	43	191,170

*New England includes Maine, New Hampshire, Vermont, Connecticut, Rhode Island, and Massachusetts. Prices subject to change.

TABLE 4.2
American Publishing Company—Metro Plan C

Due to the range of individual rates and packages, APC Metro rates are available on a per-ad basis only. Simply call or fax your ad to receive rates for the papers you're interested in.

PUBLICATION	DAILY CIRCULATION	SUNDAY CIRCULATION
Atlanta Constitution	482,251	699,172
Baltimore Sun	357,177	488,890
Boston Globe	508,867	812,021
Boston Herald	330,614	223,190
Buffalo News	305,482	382,054
Charlotte Observer	231,027	297,908
Chicago Sun-Times	531,462	537,169
Chicago Tribune	724,256	1,109,622
Cleveland Plain Dealer	410,237	545,849
Columbus Ohio Dispatch	264,601	399,494
Dallas Morning News	479,215	809,188
Denver Post	262,041	428,391
Denver Rocky Mountain News	365,480	434,177
Detroit Free Press	587,952	1,191,790
Ft. Lauderdale Sun-Sentinel	265,848	364,250
Fort Worth Star Telegram	259,328	353,520
Hartford Courant	229,284	320,132
Houston Post	296,878	336,535
Indianapolis Star	230,041	413,549
Los Angeles Times	1,164,388	1,773,876
Louisville Courier-Journal	236,103	326,868
Miami Herald	420,445	546,362
Milwaukee Journal	236,943	490,020
Minneapolis Star Tribune	412,871	685,975
Newark Star Ledger	481,027	720,174
New Orleans Times	269,639	324,997
New York Daily News	781,796	983,240
New York Times	1,201,970	1,773,876
Omaha World Herald	225,381	285,287
Orange County Register	338,453	400,880
Orlando Sentinel	271,384	376,684
Philadelphia Inquirer	548,981	977,684
Arizona Republic	390,838	603,434
Portland Oregonian	336,087	444,218
St. Louis Post-Dispatch	339,545	559,144
St. Petersburg Times	326,062	423,332
Sacramento Bee	264,259	335,113
San Diego Union	373,453	441,584

TABLE 4.2 *(continued)*

Publication	Daily Circulation	Sunday Circulation
San Francisco Chronicle	556,765	707,881
San Jose Mercury News	270,174	330,847
Seattle Times	239,476	517,742
Tampa Tribune	326,062	423,332
Washington Post	791,289	1,143,145
USA Today	1,540,698	1,903,944
Wall Street Journal	1,795,448	

State Press Associations

State press associations offer classified ad discounts of 50 percent or more. Basic ad rates are for twenty-five words or fewer, with an extra charge for additional words. Many states do not accept ads for home-business programs, lotteries, or diets. Again, rates are subject to change, so receive confirmation before placing your order. Refer to the Resource Directory for a list of state press associations.

Make Your Classified Ad Tower over the Competition

Since your ad will appear amid a sea of other classifieds, in order to achieve maximum impact two things must happen: Your ad must be seen, and it must be credible. The worst mistake you can make is to overhype your product. Your goal is to attract attention, interest, and finally action (getting them to contact you for more information).

Have you ever noticed the "disclaimers" run by editors in the classified sections? They are among the most widely read notices, and usually they aren't even selling anything. For example:

NOTICE TO READERS

In order to make a more informed decision in choosing an advance-fee broker, we suggest that you ask how long they have been in business and request a complete description of their services, including their refund policy.

TABLE 4.3
State Press Association Rates and Data

Prices are subject to change. Ad deadlines in most states are noon Tuesday, Wednesday, or Thursday.

State	Rate/ 25 Words	Extra Words	Number of Publications	Circulation
Alabama	$125.00	$6.00	93	1,010,772
Arizona	100.00	4.00	87	552,609
Arkansas	99.00	5.00	77	348,847
Colorado	99.00	4.00	101	651,018
Connecticut/ Rhode Island	55.00	5.00	42	320,250
Florida	125.00	5.00	64	1,064,400
Georgia	150.00	6.00	97	514,899
Idaho	99.00	5.00	41	202,245
Illinois	300.00	7.00	213	1,450,821
Indiana	125.00	5.00	100	934,904
Iowa	125.00	5.00	238	1,285,668
Kansas	110.00	6.00	82	326,999
Kentucky	124.00	5.00	74	937,296
Louisiana	99.00	4.00	79	549,372
Maine/Vermont	55.00	5.00	23	167,700
Massachusetts	80.00	5.00	41	502,900
Minnesota	149.00	6.00	313	2,006,656
Mississippi	99.00	5.00	62	414,980
Missouri	300.00	7.00	100	2,000,000
Montana	99.00	4.00	63	190,038
Nevada	99.00	4.00	23	359,818
New England	100.00	5.00	174	476,175
New Jersey	125.00	6.00	72	878,134
New York	180.00	7.00	184	1,071,507
New Mexico	80.00	5.00	28	202,424
North Carolina	200.00	5.00	138	1,425,451
North Dakota	95.00	4.00	95	425,753
Ohio	118.00	6.00	103	871,740
Oklahoma	175.00	7.00	110	591,051
Oregon	125.00	5.00	76	361,286
South Carolina	200.00	6.00	72	716,450
South Dakota	125.00	5.00	150	374,286
Tennessee	99.00	4.00	87	833,269
Utah	69.00	3.00	30	152,905
Virginia	175.00	6.00	73	1,397,670
West Virginia	99.00	4.00	50	559,236
Washington	129.00	4.00	111	1,092,022
Wisconsin	119.00	4.00	173	1,615,484
Wyoming	99.00	5.00	41	179,481

Check out the headline: "Notice to Readers" commands attention by appealing directly to the reader. The body of the message establishes credibility by providing "free advice" for the reader's protection. As a result, the ad leaps out at the reader, achieving maximum impact. Your ad should take the same approach. Here's an example:

ATTENTION READERS

Many home business opportunities sell information that makes money for the SELLER first and you the buyer second—if at all! Get the FACTS. Call 555-1212.

Note the similarities between the two ads. The headline grabs attention, then authority and credibility are established by providing information the reader was not aware of. The formula for successful classified advertising is:

Attention + Credibility = Response

It's well worth the extra few dollars for a centered, **BOLD, ALL CAPS HEADLINE.** Two or three words is all you need. Use power words such as "ATTENTION," "WARNING," or "BEWARE." You don't always have to use the word "Readers." Address the reader according to category, such as "Investors" or "Job Seekers." The body copy should more closely resemble a message than a sales pitch. Use brief phrases and sentences, and keep it about twenty-five words in length. The more effectively you can blend information with your message, the better your response will be.

Tips for Classified Ad Success

There's no need to reinvent the wheel; look for competitors' ads that catch your eye, and incorporate the best elements. You'll learn even more by actually responding to various ads and researching your competition. If they provide a telephone number, call and record the message on your answering machine or pocket recorder. Analyze the presentation. Order the products. Get a feel for what works. You'll be amazed at how quickly you catch on. This is a proven, enjoyable, and highly profitable system for succeeding with classified ads. Best of all, you can get started right away!

Here are three rules to remember when considering a publication to run your classified ads:

1. The publication should have a circulation of 400,000 readers or more.
2. It should have two or three pages devoted entirely to classified ads on a regular basis.
3. If you have placed ads in the publication before, those ads should have yielded twice as many orders as you needed to break even. If they did not, it may not be worth it to advertise in the publication again.

The Two-Step Sales Method

Never sell directly from a classified ad unless your product is a booklet or report that only costs two or three dollars. You just don't have the space to effectively sell the reader on the benefits of your product if it costs more than that. The purpose of a classified ad is to make the reader send for more information as quickly as possible. Ask them to write to you for free information, or call for a *recorded* message. By emphasizing that your message is recorded, you will dramatically increase your response rate, since most people would rather listen to a tape than to a live, pushy salesperson.

POWERTIP

National Mail Order Classified offers discounted rates on classified and display ads in a wide variety of national publications. They'll mail you a free package listing dozens of magazines that reach your target audience. They also offer discounts on *Best By Mail* columns that can save you big money on classified ads. Write to:

National Mail Order Classified
P.O. Box 5
Sarasota, FL 34230

POWERTIP

If you don't want to use your home address or a U.S. post office box for mail orders, use a mail outlet such as Pak-Mail or Mailboxes, Etc. Their street address becomes your street address, and your "box" number becomes a "suite" number.

Rent a voice-mail box and retrieve the responses by phone or fax, or install a second line in your home and turn your answering machine into a twenty-four-hour order desk. This is a great technique for increasing sales, since your recorded message can elaborate on your product's benefits and provide ordering details while you're off doing something else. Limit your script to two minutes or so, and speak in a clear, friendly voice. Don't try to be the overbearing announcer from those old K-Tel commercials. If you sound like Marge Simpson, you can always get a friend or local DJ to record the message.

CHAPTER 5

SELLING TO
CATALOG PUBLISHERS

Mail order by catalog continues to be a dominant marketing presence, despite the popularity of direct response, infomercials, and the Internet. Not only is mail-order shopping enjoyable and convenient, it is still the best way to reach the heartland of America: the rural consumer. In 1995, nearly seven million people bought products from the Fingerhut catalog alone.

The way catalog sales work is you supply the product while the catalog company prints a photo and description and ships orders to customers in exchange for a percentage of the retail price. Most catalog houses purchase products at wholesale discounts of 50 to 65 percent, then ship to customers directly from their warehouse. If they like your product and the discount is right, they will order anywhere from several hundred to a few thousand units. Even at a 60 percent discount you'll make a sizable profit, since you have no overhead for advertising, fulfillment, or, in some cases, shipping.

Catalogs are an excellent way to sell how-to books and tapes; they often carry books in the 8½ by 11-inch format, whereas retail stores prefer the more traditional 5½ by 8½-inch size (which are more expensive to print).

If your book or product appears in just one catalog for a single mailing, you could move a few thousand units, depending on the size of the catalog's mailing list. If your product appears in the same catalog for an entire year, you could sell 5,000, 20,000, 40,000 or more. And there are hundreds of catalogs to choose from. Talk about cost-effective, income-generating reach!

Your product doesn't have to be a how-to book or even the next *Clapper*. Cheap, easy-to-produce novelty items such as humorous T-shirts, slogans, calendars, note pads, buttons, bumper stickers, posters, and baseball caps are all proven mail-order favorites. The more topical, creative, or unique the better.

Selling Your Product to a Catalog Company

How do you capture the attention of catalog publishers? Before doing so, make sure that you are in a position to carry several hundred to a few thousand units of your product. Then compile a list of catalogs best suited to your product (see the references at the end of this chapter). The next step is to send all the catalogs on your list a promotional package. Address all correspondence to the attention of the *merchandising department* or *director of merchandising*. Your promotional package should consist of the following:

- Sales literature and ad copy: This should include everything you have that illustrates the value of your product. Document the publicity you've received, sales figures from previous successful advertising campaigns, and so on. If you're just starting out, list the benefits and features and emphasize the uniqueness of your product. What problem does it solve? How will it enrich consumers' lives?
- Product photo: Shoot the picture yourself or hire a professional photographer. If you do it yourself, use a 35mm camera and stick to basics; focus on the product. Study existing catalogs for ideas. Send individual 5 by 7-inch enlargements. Some catalogs do the photography themselves from your sample for a one-time fee of about forty-five dollars.
- Price discount: The deeper the discount, the better your chances of placement. When calculating discounts, consider your manufacturing costs per unit, and remember

that manufacturing and shipping will be your only costs at this point. Catalog houses prosper by offering their customers below-retail prices, while simultaneously absorbing substantial overhead for printing, mailing list rentals, postage, and warehouse inventory. How do they do it? *Volume.*

The usual discount for untested, first-time products is 60 to 70 percent below retail. On big-ticket items (sixty dollars and up), the discount drops to about 50 percent. Of course, you gain the advantage if you have a proven or potential hit. It's your job to convince them that you do. Don't be greedy; remember the goal is volume sales. Most catalog companies buy in gross lots of 144 units. Structure your discounts according to gross, with incremental discounts of five, ten, and twenty gross, and so on.

- Payment terms: Don't expect to receive payment in advance until you have a proven winner. The industry standard is net thirty days (paid in full thirty days after receipt of invoice), with a two percent discount if paid within ten days.
- Freight terms: You can either pay freight yourself, or factor it into your discount schedule. Experiment and be flexible; you can always make adjustments as you learn the ropes.
- Product sample: Make two lists of catalog companies—your primary and your secondary targets. Primary targets should specialize in your type of product, while secondary targets should sell a more general list of products. Send product samples to your primary targets only. The others will request a sample if they are interested. Include a response card in your mailing to the secondary list in order to make it more convenient for them to respond.

Setting Up Business with a Catalog Publisher

Receiving a merchandising data form from a catalog company means that the company is seriously interested in your product. However, this is not a commitment to buy, so be sure to sell your product well on the merchandising data form. Fill out the form completely, include any additional information they request, make a copy for your records, and return it immediately by overnight courier.

The next step is a purchase order. If you receive one of these, you're in! Ship your product immediately; there's no time to waste. On initial orders, you might have thirty days to get your product from manufacturer to catalog house. Reorders are almost always a rush job, so it's important to reinvest your profits to ensure that you always have between 500 and 1,000 units ready to go on a moment's notice. The best scenario is to have your manufacturer ship the product directly to the catalog house either prepaid or collect, according to the terms of your agreement.

A fact of life in the catalog business is the excruciatingly long lead time. Merchandise is acquired and art design and layout are completed months in advance of the actual catalog release date. Christmas catalogs may be prepared as early as April or May. It could be weeks or months before you receive a response, positive or negative. While competition for space in a widely distributed catalog is fierce, those same catalogs are fiercely searching for new products. Every catalog company strives to be the first to introduce a hot new product.

Preparation, creativity, and persistence are crucial in the catalog business. If your product isn't placed in a catalog immediately, keep trying. Use the catalogs you do get into to attract interest from others. Be persistent. And even when it is placed, don't stop marketing your product at that point. Always follow through with updates of any recent publicity, sales figures, or endorsements you've acquired since the original mailing.

After you've cut your deal and shipped your product, the fun begins. Time to chill out and wait for the checks to arrive! As long as your product is selling, the catalogs will be back for more. Reorders can occur on a monthly or bi-monthly basis, depending on the season.

Finally, don't be intimidated. It gets easier after the first deal or two. You'll overcome your initial uncertainty as you go. Mail-order catalogs can be an extremely rewarding part of your marketing agenda. Remember, a successful mail-order product opens doors to the big leagues: the home shopping networks and the ultimate money machine, retail!

> **POWERTIP**
>
> An excellent way to expose your book or product to the catalog indus-
> try is a review in *Direct Marketing Magazine,* the bible of the catalog
> industry. A favorable review in Peter Hoke's "Friday Report" could gen-
> erate a stream of inquiries. Send a news release and product sample by
> rush or overnight carrier to:
>
> **Peter Hoke, Publisher**
> *Direct Marketing Magazine*
> 24 Seventh Street
> Garden City, NY 11535

How to Find Catalog Publishers

The National Directory of Catalogs is *the* catalog reference
source: more than 800 pages packed with thousands of catalog listings, including address, best contact, product line,
circulation, and general information. It also includes
tips on selling to catalog houses. The directory is updated
annually, so be sure to call for the current price. It is
published by:

Oxbridge Communications Inc.
150 Fifth Avenue
New York, NY 10011
(800) 955-0231

With *The Catalog of Catalogs* you only get straight listings,
but it sells for only about twenty dollars. It is available in
bookstores or by writing to:

The Catalog of Catalogs
1020 North Broadway, Suite 111
Milwaukee, WI 53202
(414) 272-9977

Catalogs Worldwide is a free publication listing hundreds
of catalogs. Get a copy by writing to:

Interstate Publications
P.O. Drawer 19689
Houston, TX 77224

POWERTIP

The most comprehensive source about catalogs, *The Mail Order Business Directory* contains more than 12,000 of the most active mail-order and catalog houses in the U.S. that together distribute several hundred million catalogs annually. Information is listed by categories, names of buyers or executives in charge, phone numbers, sales volume, and products carried. This directory also contains more than 1,000 leading Canadian and foreign mail-order companies, and includes a concise guide to selling to the mail-order market. The price is ninety-five dollars for the 500-page 18th edition (1996), available from:

B. Klein Publications
P.O. Box 6578
Delray Beach, FL 33482
(561) 496-3316

CHAPTER 6

FAIRS, TRADE SHOWS, AND FLEA MARKETS: CONSUMERS, CONTACTS, AND CASH

The knowledge of the world is only to be acquired in the world, and not in a closet.

Lord Chesterfield

ONE OF THE BEST WAYS to simultaneously test your product and make valuable industry contacts is to take your product "on tour." Fairs are teeming with people who are carrying spendable cash. You could easily earn six figures a year selling at the hundreds of fairs held across the U.S. during summer and autumn, and take the rest of the year off. Many entrepreneurs have become millionaires from selling at fairs alone. There are also a variety of special-interest trade shows held year-round.

Whatever your product, idea, or service, there's probably a show for it. Just load up your car or truck and book a motel room. The hours can be long, but you'll be too busy raking in the cash to notice! Best of all, you're the boss, calling the shots and picking your spots.

Depending on size, renting a space at a ten-day fair can cost between $500 and $1,000, or $50 to $100 per day. A bargain, considering you can make a few thousand dollars a day. If you limit the cost of your product to 20 percent of the sale price, the profit potential can be startling!

Fairs and trade shows also provide excellent preparation for the world of electronic marketing (radio and television advertising). You can demonstrate and test your product midstream, something you couldn't afford to risk in an expensive print or TV ad campaign. You'll sharpen your sales skills, gain immediate valuable insight from consumers, and make influential contacts. You can even sell your product to fellow entrepreneurs at a discount, so that they can sell at other fairs and shows around the country. The possibilities are limitless.

You can get a list of fairs and trade shows in your area from your local phone book, chamber of commerce, or industry publications such as *Trade Show and Exhibit Schedules* and *Successful Meetings Magazine* (see the Resource Directory). Next, contact the fair managers for an application form and layout of available locations. Always check attendance figures from the previous year's fair before you commit. Concentrate on established fairs and shows with proven attendance. *Never buy space at a first-time, unproven fair.*

Obtain as much information as possible. How far will the product booths be from the main flow of traffic? Are the booths indoors? Is there air conditioning? Will people be ducking inside to escape the heat? By visualizing the setup, the pertinent questions will come to you. The best way to familiarize yourself with a show from a vendor's perspective is to visit one or two and take notes. You'll also find plenty of ideas for the next crucial element: your booth.

Your booth or display area is your storefront, and it should be as inviting and attractive as possible. Have a sign or banner made up and map out the lighting. Of course, your best advertising is your product. Stack it up behind your booth and position samples in front. Set out plenty of copies of your sales literature for people to take away with them. Hire a model to give away balloons or candy. Again, you'll get plenty of ideas by scouting a few fairs and shows before taking the plunge. State and county fairs generally draw the biggest crowds, but don't overlook the shows that target your particular field, such as business, auto, or health and diet shows.

Your costs will consist of vendor fees, a hotel room, and meals, which are all tax-deductible. Many experienced veterans of fairs, trade shows, and even seminars combine work with a vacation and legally deduct their expenses!

Trade Shows

The fundamental difference between a fair and a trade show is the clientele. At fairs you will need more product, since you're dealing directly with consumers. Trade shows are frequented by manufacturers, retail buyers, and other industry bigwigs, which can lead to valuable networking opportunities and contacts. There are seminars offered by leaders in the field, as well as the opportunity to brainstorm and share ideas with fellow entrepreneurs. Often, the contacts you make with influential distributors, sales representatives, and other decision-makers can be more advantageous to you than actual sales.

Trade shows are more flamboyant than fairs, and competition is fierce. The best locations are usually reserved for corporations and returning exhibitors, so you'll have to use every creative tactic at your disposal in order to make an impact. Once again, the best source of ideas is the shows themselves.

Put together press kits for distribution to the media and other important contacts, and find out if there is a press room where you can leave a stack of your kits.

Another significant difference between fairs and trade shows involves your product. Since you'll be taking orders to be shipped later, you only need to bring a few samples to a trade show. On the final day of a show, many vendors sell their samples at a discount to avoid having to lug them home. Remember to focus on established shows with proven attendance records.

Flea Markets

Imagine sitting on a bale of hay, a piece of straw pinched between your teeth, enjoying the brisk outdoor air—and making more money in a weekend than many people make all week at their jobs! Flea markets will always be an integral part of Americana, offering entrepreneurs a variety of fun and exciting ways to make $4,000 to $10,000 per month, then take weekdays off.

Get started by deciding on a solid line of products to sell. *Closeout News* is an excellent source of wholesale, close-out, and other discount merchandise that can be obtained for pennies on the dollar (contact information appears below). You'll find excellent deals on almost anything you can think of: novelty items, jewelry, tools, sporting goods, telephones, collectibles, electronics, and more. Some of the prices will astonish you.

Most states require that you have a business license and/or seller's permit in order to offer merchandise for sale to the public; these usually cost about twenty dollars. Once you've obtained your seller's permit, have a banner or sign made, and scout the popular flea markets in your area. The majority rent booths to vendors for twenty to fifty dollars per day on a first-come, first-served basis. It's worth getting there at six o'clock on the day of the sale in order to get a good spot.

Get a copy of *Closeout News* and highlight the products that interest you and (most importantly) will sell. The items mentioned in the previous paragraph are all good flea-market sellers. One company even offers a line of "As Seen on TV" products. These can be terrific items to sell, since millions of dollars have already gone into advertising them to the public. You can pick them up at close-out prices, mark them up from 100 to 400 percent, and still sell them for below TV cost. And unlike ordering from TV, there are no shipping and handling charges or four- to six-week to waits for the stuff to arrive!

The possibilities are limitless. I heard of one fellow who picked up a load of AT&T cordless telephones through *Closeout News* for ten dollars each, then turned around and sold them to a local AT&T Phone Center for twenty-five dollars each! Not bad. Flea markets are an excellent way to earn the part-time cash you need to finance your full-time aspirations, leaving your weekdays free to write, create, and brainstorm.

Industry Publications

Here is a list of some industry publications about fairs, trade shows, and flea markets:

Closeout News
728 East Eighth Street, Suite 1
Holland, MI 49423
(616) 392-9687

Fair Times
P.O. Box 692
Abington, PA 19001

Marketer's Forum
Forum Publications
383 East Main Street
Centerport, NY 11721
(516) 754-5000
(Information about flea markets)

Trade Show Bureau
1660 Lincoln Street, Suite 2080
Denver, CO 80264
(303) 860-7626

The following are companies that sell equipment for trade shows, from display booths to lighting and accessories. Contact them for a free catalog:

The Godfrey Group, Inc.
P.O. Box 90008
Raleigh, NC 27675
(919) 544-6504

Nomadic Display
7400 Fullerton Road
Springfield, VA 22153
(800) 732-9395

Professional Exhibits and Graphics
3104 O Street, #341
Sacramento, CA 95816
(916) 498-1183

CHAPTER 7

ELECTRONIC RETAIL: THE FUTURE OF DIRECT MARKETING

When you are aspiring to the highest place, it is honorable to reach the second or even the third rank.

Cicero

ELECTRONIC RETAIL IS ESSENTIALLY the use of technology to market products in a way that makes it easy for customers to immediately respond by placing a telephone order. Because the vast majority of our purchases are "impulse buys," the more convenient you make it for consumers to order your widget, the more successful you'll be. This is known as "direct-response" advertising.

Inbound Telemarketing with Your Own Toll-Free Number

The wave of the future is selling via telephone, and the time to get involved is now. A great way to sell product is to obtain a toll-free phone number and hire an *inbound company* to handle the orders. Inbound companies are businesses set up to process phone orders for other businesses—in other

75

words, a customer calling your toll-free number will talk to a telemarketer at the inbound company who will take care of the sale for you, leaving you free to concentrate on other things (see Figure 7.1).

Toll-free numbers have become an essential part of retail business in the nineties. Offering your customers the convenience of toll-free ordering can boost mail-order sales by 20 percent or more. Increased popularity and affordability has made it possible for a business of any size to set up a toll-free number.

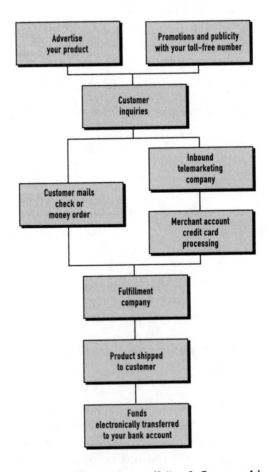

Figure 7.1 *Electronic retail "cash-flow machine"*

If you hire an inbound company, every time a customer dials your toll-free number, your product data will automatically pop up on the telemarketer's computer screen. The data includes information about your product, price, shipping and handling, delivery time, and your customer service number for inquiries (possibly your home office phone). You should write this script yourself to be sure the information is complete and that all potential customer questions are covered. After your script has been entered into the company's database, ask to receive a printout for proofing.

When someone places an order, the operator takes down the customer's name, address, phone number, and credit card or checking account information (expect approximately 10 percent of your customers to pay by check). You are charged a usage fee of about ninety-five cents per minute whether the caller places an order or not, so it's imperative that you oversee the script and make sure the telemarketers are answering queries and taking orders as efficiently as possible.

After the order has been processed, the inbound company will send you a copy for your records and fulfillment. If you are working with a manufacturer that also provides order fulfillment, the inbound company forwards the orders to the manufacturer or fulfillment company, which in turn ships your product directly to the customer. Such an arrangement not only eliminates the cost of shipping between manufacturer and fulfillment house, it shortens turnaround time on future product runs.

Your inbound company will inform you of the number of calls received per day. This can include inquiries in addition to orders. An "aborted calls" report provides essential feedback on the calls from people who didn't order, and why. Were they referred to your customer service number for additional information? How long were they on the line? This information tells you whether your script is working or requires modification.

About 5 percent of your credit card orders will be rejected. When this occurs, the inbound company will contact the customer and offer the option of paying by check. Unless your inbound company includes check processing, customers paying by check will need to mail payment either to you or to your fulfillment company for processing. A growing number of inbound companies perform automatic checking account debits.

When the orders have been fulfilled and credit card fees deducted, the inbound company deposits your profits directly into your bank account. What could be more efficient and convenient?

CHOOSING A GOOD INBOUND COMPANY

The best source for finding an inbound company is *Response TV* magazine (see the Resource Directory). Get a subscription, make a list of companies, and contact them for an information kit that describes their range of services, how much they charge per minute, transaction and processing fees, and order fulfillment. Take the time to do a little research and make a few calls, and you'll undoubtedly find an inbound company to fit your individual requirements and budget.

Of course, you could always get a toll-free number linked to your home office and process orders yourself, but who wants to sit by the phone all day? Hire an employee? Outsourcing is the key to success in business. Even large corporations are finally waking up to what successful entrepreneurs have known for years—farm out as much of the work as possible, and keep your operation lean, mean, and nimble. If you hire someone to come in and work for you, you become liable for health and employment insurance, and all the headaches that come with being an employer. When you outsource, you can write it all off as a business expense.

Here are some inbound telemarketing companies to consider. Call and ask for a list of fees and services to help you tailor a package that meets your needs.

Advantage Communications: (800) 446-1199
Alert Communications: (800) 333-7772
All-West Communications: (800) 532-5255
Answer All America: (800) 356-5324
Matrixx Marketing: (800) 543-6423
Telenational Marketing: (800) 333-6106

Telesystems, Inc.: (800) 622-0190
Telnet Systems: (800) 456-6546

While a standard voice-mail box can be a cheaper alternative to an 800 number (twenty to thirty dollars per month through a private local company), there are drawbacks. Extra work is required to process orders yourself, and many customers may be unwilling to pay for a long-distance call to your number. Again, it is possible to get your own toll-free number, but it's much easier to outsource, especially when the orders really start coming in. Some telemarketing companies can set you up with a voice-mail box via an 800 number. You can record a message up to three minutes long providing details about your offer, then either record orders or transfer the caller to a live operator.

MERCHANT ACCOUNTS AND INDEPENDENT SALES ORGANIZATIONS

Before you can accept credit card orders over the telephone, you'll need a merchant account in order to process them. These accounts make it possible to both process credit card orders and perform automatic checking account debits. When a telemarketing company takes an order, the order is forwarded by fax or Electronic Data File Transfer to a credit card processing company. Credit card companies handle payment processing on all the major cards twenty-four hours a day, seven days a week. They provide customized reports, and electronically deposit the funds into your bank account the next day. Many companies will not transfer funds until the order is shipped, in which case proof of shipment from your fulfillment company is required before funds are electronically deposited to your account.

Independent sales organizations (ISOs) are companies that have been authorized by credit card companies to "lease" their merchant accounts to small businesses for a fee. Call for information:

Bancard Trust Company: (818) 999-3333
Card Acceptance Corporation: (619) 530-1770
Continental Bankard Services: (213) 488-9657

National Association of Credit Card Merchants:
(407) 737-7500
United Merchant Services: (213) 257-1818
U.S. Merchant Services: (212) 818-1807

Order Fulfillment

While some telemarketing companies also provide fulfillment, you might find it more cost-effective to keep this part
of your operation close to the location of your business.
Fulfillment is a vital part of your cash-flow machine, saving
you valuable time and labor at a cost of approximately 8
percent of your total overhead.

If you use a fulfillment company, it will work in conjunc-
tion with your inbound company, receiving daily orders and
reports, and promptly shipping your product to customers.
They also make sure you have sufficient inventory on hand.

A common mistake beginners make is to try to handle
fulfillment in-house. There are more productive ways to spend
your time than tediously packaging, labeling, and shipping
packages. Then there's the tricky business of tracking customer orders. Unless your package is unusually large or
cumbersome, shipping through a fulfillment house should
only cost between two dollars and five dollars per package.
Check the Yellow Pages under "Fulfillment" or "Mail Order
Houses," or consult trade magazines such as *Response TV.*

INVENTORY AND THE THIRTY-DAY LAW

FTC regulations require that products be shipped to consumers no later than thirty days from the order date, unless

POWERTIP

If you're just starting out and are looking for a turnkey, inexpensive
toll-free number and merchant account, I recommend Mountain West
Communications in Hotchkiss, Colorado. They'll set you up with a dedicated 800 number for about $500. Transactions are processed via their
merchant account for a small additional fee. The staff is friendly and
helpful, and they take a genuine interest in your success. To receive an
information kit, call (800) 642-9378.

otherwise stated ("allow four to six weeks for delivery"). If you promise delivery in thirty days and are unable to meet that deadline, you must send a postcard informing customers of the delay, the reason for the delay, and the new delivery date, and give them the option to cancel the order. The FTC has been known to levy hefty fines for failure to comply with this regulation. Always track your inventory and make sure your fulfillment company notifies you before you run out of stock.

Selling Information via 800 Numbers

The difference between an 800 number and a 900 number is in the billing procedure. Whereas with 900 numbers the caller is charged for the call, with 800 numbers the information provider pays for the call. Cunning entrepreneurs have developed a way to side-step the stigma associated with 900 numbers and reduce costs by selling information through an 800 number and charging the caller directly. (For details on 900 numbers, see Chapter 12.)

Here's how it works: you advertise the 800 number just as you would a 900 number. Callers receive free introductory information leading them to a menu-driven format that guides them to their specific area of interest. Before they can access this information, they must enter their credit card number over the phone for approval on an automated system provided by your service bureau. You get immediate electronic access to the funds, and since there's no need for the phone company or service bureau to collect for the calls, you avoid the service charges. When using this method it is extremely important to provide genuine, reliable information of value. This will minimize refunds resulting from customer dissatisfaction.

Simply choose a service bureau that provides the necessary hardware to process your calls (see Chapter 12). Prepare your script, then advertise your 800 number with classified, print, radio, or TV ads. You can even negotiate per-inquiry agreements, offering a percentage of the revenue generated from calls to your line (see Chapter 8).

Home Shopping Networks

While mail-order catalog shopping is still the undisputed champion when it comes to sales volume, home shopping TV networks are a force to be reckoned with. They boast over six million viewers who purchase more than $2.5 billion in merchandise annually. In 1994, QVC (Quality, Variety, and Convenience) alone did $1.2 billion in sales—as much as the entire infomercial industry. Home shopping networks are the mail-order catalogs of the information age. Home shopping is enjoyable, reliable, and convenient. The sales potential is explosive; a hot product can sell 10,000 units or more in as little as fifteen minutes of air time!

The home shopping networks are interested in a variety of unique, quality merchandise that can be easily demonstrated on-camera. They also like new product launches. Since home shopping programming is theme-driven, products are chosen according to how well they fit in. For example, QVC does not accept personalized merchandise, children's wear, furs, guns, or service-related programs.

The quickest route to the home shopping networks is with a product that has had previous television exposure (short-form commercials and infomercials). However, this isn't the only way. Each network has its own Vendor Relations department. Contact them and ask for a Product Information Form. Fill it out and return it, along with a photo of your product (samples are discouraged). The odds are long, but definitely worth a shot. Three-quarters of the more than 1,000 product sheets received every week are rejected. The other 25 percent receive a second look.

As with catalogs and retailers, the home shopping networks purchase products at a discount and resell them directly to their customers. Upon preliminary approval, a product must pass rigorous quality assurance requirements. It must also be individually packaged and labeled for shipping in accordance with the network's seven-day customer delivery guarantee.

In 1993, Stan Herman took his line of chenille robes to QVC and sold 9,600 units in twelve minutes. By the end of the day, he had sold 22,300 for a total of $661,000. If you believe your product has home shopping potential, get a Product Information Form right away. You never know where it may lead!

Although there are several smaller home shopping networks across the nation, the two largest and best are:

The Home Shopping Network
11831 Thirtieth Court North
St. Petersburg, FL 33716
(813) 572-8585

QVC
1365 Enterprise Drive
Westchester, PA 19308
(800) 345-1515

Wholesale Clubs

If you have a quality product at a low price and are having a difficult time getting the attention of retail chains, try wholesale outlets such as Costco, the Price Club, and Sam's Wholesale Club. They offer a 10 percent markup on merchandise, spacious aisles, and plenty of shelf space. They are also easier to deal with than major retailers, since they're not as concerned with national TV exposure.

CHAPTER 8

PER-INQUIRY ADVERTISING: HOW TO GET RADIO AND TELEVISION ADS WITH LITTLE OR NO MONEY

For continued success, study and prepare to accomplish future objectives.

Harry F. Banks

YOU'VE SEEN THE COMMERCIALS: *Hooked on Phonics, BreathAsure, RolyKit,* and *Miracle Mop,* to name just a few. These entrepreneurs must have invested tens of thousands of dollars in advertising to launch their products, right? Actually, many began with little or no advertising capital at all. An increasing number of new products are being marketed on a *per-inquiry* (PI) basis, and enjoy phenomenal success in a short period of time. Per-inquiry is the term for an agreement between an advertiser and a radio or television station in which, instead of receiving payment up front, the station's sales manager agrees to run commercials in exchange for a percentage of the sales. Stations then use PI commercials to fill unsold air time.

By taking advantage of the millions of dollars in unsold, unused air time on radio, TV, and cable stations across the country, entrepreneurs have blanketed the marketplace.

With over 11,000 radio stations, 5,000 cable stations, and 2,000 network affiliates nationwide, it is simply impossible to sell all the available space. And this ad time constitutes "perishable inventory," similar to vacant rooms in hotels or empty seats on airlines. Cable TV is an excellent medium for PI. New cable channels are being added all the time. And the more cable channels there are, the more available air time goes unsold.

Corporate advertisers and entrepreneurs have learned to hitch a ride on this unsold air time; they run their commercials in exchange for a percentage of the price of each unit sold (usually between 25 and 35 percent).

Hooked on Phonics is an excellent example of the power of PI. John Shanahan introduced this reading program in 1986, first on radio and later on TV. Revenues went from $100,000 in 1987 to sales of $150 million by 1994. Anthony Raissen launched his natural breath freshener, *BreathAsure,* on a single Los Angeles radio station, and made so much money that he soon became their biggest advertiser!

Launching a Successful Per-Inquiry Campaign

There is a galaxy of opportunity available to entrepreneurs who know how to market products by electronic retail. The keys to a successful PI campaign are a hot product, an established electronic marketing network (inbound toll-free telemarketing, credit card processing, and fulfillment), a professional presentation, and a basic knowledge of broadcast sales (see *Making Successful Radio Buys*; information provided at the end of this chapter). Getting started is as easy as producing a sixty- or ninety-second radio commercial and then contacting the general sales manager (GSM) of your local AM news/talk radio station.

Local radio is a perfect way to sharpen your skills at minimal risk, and the news/talk format has a much higher listener attention span than do music stations. The key is to convince the GSM that your product will sell enough to make money for the station, eventually putting you in the position to become a regular advertising client. After all, when your product takes off, you'll want to keep the cash flow rolling in with additional ads in higher-reach time slots ("dayparts"), such as morning or afternoon commute hours ("drive-time").

The industry standard for PI is between 25 and 35 percent of the sale price of each unit. For example, if your product sells for $19.95, the station's percentage would be five to seven dollars per unit sold. The disadvantage of running commercials in unsold air time is the lack of control; your ads run at the station's discretion. Negotiate maximum reach and frequency, in order to expose your message to the largest possible audience. After all, it's in the station's best interest to help you generate as many sales as possible. Remember, you're only using PI to get you to the point where you can afford to buy additional commercials and schedule them in better time slots.

Getting Your Ad on the Air

Start by producing a sixty- or ninety-second commercial, or "spot," that includes your toll-free number for ordering or for additional information. You can produce the commercial yourself or have the station do it for you. Ask for a schedule of how often and at what times your commercial will air.

Your telemarketing company will track the number of orders and provide both you and the GSM with a weekly or daily printout of orders generated by the ad. You then fulfill orders and pay the station its percentage. These "third party" printouts are the station's guarantee of an independent, accurate report.

You must be professional in all of your dealings, and pay your "partners" on time every month. If your product is successful on smaller stations, ask for a letter of endorsement from the GSM documenting your success. This will demonstrate to other stations both the marketability of your product and your professionalism. The profit potential can be truly staggering as you add more and more stations to your network!

The print media have been slow to accept PI, but with rising costs and increased competition, it won't be long before they catch up. PI is a classic win-win situation because it really works.

The following summary of steps will get you well on your way:

1. Establish your electronic marketing network: toll-free number, merchant account, and fulfillment routine.
2. Produce a sixty- or ninety-second radio commercial for your product. You can get a local ad agency or radio station to do this for as little as $120.
3. Contact local AM news/talk radio stations in your area. Try to bypass the regular salespeople (Account Executives, or AEs); ask to speak directly with the General Sales Manager.
4. Send the GSM a proposal letter (see the sample included in this chapter) along with a media kit and press release. Convince the GSM of the sales potential of your product and of your desire to become a long-term advertiser on the station.
5. Start by offering the station 20 percent of gross sales. Go as high as 30 percent, depending on the number of commercials you'll receive and when they'll run.
6. Ask the sales manager for an anticipated schedule of when your commercials will air.
7. Keep an accurate account of orders generated by each station. Process and fulfill orders, and pay the stations promptly each month.
8. Document your success. Get letters of reference from your stations. Use these endorsement letters to multiply your network of radio stations.
9. Invest your profits, and expand into television advertising. Produce a TV commercial or infomercial, incorporating testimonials from your radio campaign. Talk to production companies that specialize in electronic retail (get a subscription to *Response TV*; see references at the end of this chapter). This is where things can really get exciting, as you go from local cable companies to national networks, and perhaps even to home shopping networks and retail stores!

The costs involved in PI advertising include:

- Commercial production
- Copies (dubs) of your commercial

- Toll-free number and merchant account setup fees
- Shipping (spots, news releases, and product samples)
- Fax and long-distance charges (calling stations, developing your strategic network)

Tips for Creating Hot Radio and TV Commercials

What is written and what is spoken are as different as Swahili and Beethoven.

Gerry Spence

- Develop an attention-grabbing, unique selling position that enhances the health, wealth, or happiness of your target consumer.
- Get immediate attention with a question. Address a specific need, and pile on the benefits and features.
- Use action verbs and phrases. Stick with the action, and avoid the abstraction.
- Use superlatives like *"Revolutionary New Offer," "Miracle," "Free Bonus," "Call Now,"* etc.
- Quality wars are better than price wars. Focus on benefits and features without cheapening the perception of your product. Emphasize quality and value while remaining competitive.
- Edit, edit, edit! Stick to the facts. Sixty seconds only gives you about ninety words.
- Innovate; be fresh and exciting.
- Use testimonials.
- Include a free bonus.
- Urge customers to write down your toll-free number, have a credit card ready, and *order now!*
- Get plenty of feedback. Test your offer, price points, bonus, and other aspects of your offer.

How to Overcome Objections when Negotiating PI Deals

Expect some initial resistance from some stations that prefer you to pay in cash. After all, the ad salespeople work on a commission basis. Even if you get rejected several times, stick to your guns. Don't take it personally. Usually it isn't the deal itself they're rejecting, just what they know about it so far. Dig in, and provide more benefits and features until they come around. The following pointers may help you:

- Demonstrate demand for your product.
- Include endorsement letters from successful campaigns.
- Indicate your desire to become a loyal, regular advertiser on the station.
- Promise (and deliver) accurate daily or weekly sales reports to the sales manager.
- Provide a refundable deposit against sales if necessary.

Broadcast advertising is different from print advertising. Learn the terminology (see the end of this chapter for helpful resources) and talk the talk. These dynamic strategies combined with the right product can lead to unbelievable wealth.

John Shanahan *(Hooked on Phonics),* Joy Mangano *(Miracle Mop),* Joe Sugarman *(Blu-Blocker* sunglasses), and many other multimillionaires were once where you are today, with only a dream—and the determination to make it come true!

Infomercials

Think of infomercials as the electronic equivalent of mail order. They allow you to combine an abundance of information about your product with convenient, risk-free ordering. For those who got in on the ground floor, the early days of infomercials were a bonanza, and fortunes were made literally overnight. As an increasing number of players entered the fray, advertising rates on the networks and in large markets skyrocketed. Fortune 500 corporations soon got into the act, buying up time at these inflated rates without blinking. As a result, many independent entrepreneurs were priced out of the market.

Every station has its own policy and rate schedule. Infomercial time makes up approximately 5 percent of a

Sample PI Sales Letter

URGENT! Please Hand-Deliver To: [General Sales Manager]

We Would Like to Write a Huge Check to Your Advertising Sales Department Every Month!

[Open with a short paragraph describing your product.]

We believe that [product's] unique selling position and competitive price will appeal to a large segment of your audience. We are interested in establishing a long-term partnership with your station, and have an exciting opportunity that we hope will make you a cornerstone of our advertising network.

Per-Inquiry (PI) advertising has enjoyed remarkable success on radio and television since its inception a few years ago. In fact, when *BreathAsure* was introduced via PI on KFI Los Angeles, it became the biggest advertising client on the station in just a few months! Success stories of the power of PI continue to mount (*Hooked on Phonics, Blu-Blocker* sunglasses, *Thighmaster,* etc.).

Here's how it works. We provide a ninety-second [or sixty-second] ad for [product] with an 800 number and operator number. You run the ad whenever you have unsold space. We write you a check at the end of each month at the rate of ten dollars for each item sold. For example, if 1 percent of 100,000 listeners order the product, we'll cut you a check for $10,000 each month. The more orders we receive, the bigger the check we write you—each and every month—just for allowing us to "hitch a ride" on your unsold ad space.

Many of your repeat advertisers continue to prove that your listeners are highly responsive income-opportunity buyers. However, you have no way of benefiting from their success beyond your (deeply discounted) repeat rates. We know that your listeners are smart enough to recognize the unique selling position and superior benefits of [product] when compared with similar products.

Incidentally, the 800 operator number will be yours exclusively, so we'll always provide you with an accurate count of the responses received from your station.

Please sign the attached agreement and fax or mail it back to us today. As soon as we receive it, we will send you a tape of our radio spot. Incidentally, timing of ad placement is entirely at your discretion. This is absolutely a win-win opportunity with ZERO RISK. If you have any questions, please don't hesitate to contact me directly.

[your name and return address here]

station's available inventory, usually late at night, and during weekend mornings and afternoons. The law of supply and demand gives them the luxury of charging whatever they wish. It can easily cost $75,000 or more just to produce an infomercial. For every infomercial that makes money, many more fail. However, fortunes will continue to be made in spite of the odds. Infomercial time can be purchased for as little as $1,000. In larger markets, the cost balloons to between $10,000 and $50,000.

Buy small, start with just a few stations, test your product, and roll the profits into better time slots. Cautiously expand to four or five additional markets. Always play it safe until you've achieved genuine momentum.

To assess the profitability of your infomercial, deduct your advertising and manufacturing costs from the selling price of each item. For example, if your advertising cost is $1,000 and you sell 100 units, it cost you $10 in advertising to sell them. If your price point is $39.95 and it costs you $10 to sell them and another $10 to manufacture them, you've got a winner!

Short-form advertising and infomercials are the best way to get the attention of home shopping networks, catalogs, and national retail buyers for chains such as Wal-Mart, Sears, Target, and Costco. This is where the real money is. Exposure from radio and TV advertising can open doors to retail that might otherwise be impossible to crack.

If you have a great product for radio or television and are looking for a strategic partner, get in touch with an "infomercial marketing company." You'll find their ads in magazines such as *Response TV*. If one of these companies likes your idea, they will put up the cash for a short-form spot or infomercial, and even purchase the air time. However just like a book publisher, they also expect most of the profits. If you're more comfortable staying behind the scenes, taking a 5 or 10 percent royalty might be the way to go. But remember, infomercials have the power to sell millions of dollars in product quickly, so you could be signing away a fortune.

When partnering with an infomercial marketing company, the more expertise and money you bring to the table, the larger your share of the profits will be. You'll also retain more creative control over the project.

Here are the names of a few infomercial and product marketing companies:

> Fredericksen Television, Inc.: (703) 560-8290
> Inphomation Communications, Inc.: (410) 649-1000
> Integrated Communications Network: (305) 530-0200
> National Media Corporation: (800) 504-5004
> Positive Response Television Media: (818) 380-6930
> Product Information Network: (800) 727-5663

Excellent Sources for Electronic Marketing Information

Making Successful Radio Buys: This twenty-eight-page salesperson's booklet will help you understand terminology, math, usage statistics, and scheduling, as well as which stations are the best and why. Available for $6 from:

National Association of Broadcasters (NAB)
1771 N Street
Washington, DC 20036
(800) 368-5644

M Street Radio Directory: Complete listings of AM and FM radio stations in the U.S. and Canada. Includes addresses, phone numbers, program formats, and ratings. Available for $39 from the NAB address above.

Response TV: Recognized as the bible of the electronic marketing industry, this magazine includes information on TV commercial/infomercial production, consultants, telemarketing/fulfillment companies, and much more. The annual subscription rate is $39 for twelve issues; available from:

Response TV Magazine
201 Sandpointe Avenue, #600
Santa Ana, CA 72707
(800) 346-0085 ext. 477

CHAPTER 9

FREE PUBLICITY: CASHING IN ON AMERICA'S RAVENOUS MEDIA

MARKETING A PRODUCT or service on a limited budget is the biggest challenge facing the beginning entrepreneur. Generating free publicity to ignite sales is an approach used by professionals and beginners alike. The most fascinating example of this process is the story of the Pet Rock. Ad man Gary Dahl turned a seemingly ridiculous concept into a personal fortune—entirely through free publicity. What began as coverage in the local newspaper turned into a half-page feature article in *Time* magazine. Dahl found a manufacturer to package and ship his rock-in-a-box, and sold more than a million at a net profit of a dollar each!

There are many stories of average people who made a fortune with their ideas thanks to free publicity. A retiree made more than $100,000 selling copies of an eighteenth-century wedding certificate that had been hanging on his kitchen wall. It all started with free publicity in his local paper, and the public ate it up. A veterinarian made an inexpensive home video showing dog owners what to do to save their pet in an emergency. He mailed off a few press releases, and sold hundreds of copies via the resulting free publicity.

You can see this free advertising in action every day by simply opening a newspaper or magazine. Editorial content is more widely read and is considered to be more believable than advertisements. This explains the increasing number of "advertorials"—or ads that are disguised as news articles. The television cousin of the advertorial is the infomercial.

It's no secret that reviews sell products and books, but feature articles sell even more. Many reviewers print news releases verbatim. Editors may only use one release out of every ten they receive, but news releases make up about 25 percent of the editorial space in many newspapers and magazines. In smaller publications, the percentage can go even higher.

There are two kinds of reviews. A *summary* review describes the product or book without offering an editorial opinion. An *evaluative* review expresses a positive or negative opinion, and compares a product with others in the field. A book critic will probably read your book, whereas a book reviewer will probably only check the table of contents and your news release, so the release has to be good.

You might be thinking to yourself, "I couldn't possibly write a news release." *Au contraire.* Anyone can put together a one- or two-page, double-spaced release; it's just like the book reports you did in school. Editors and TV and radio news directors are always looking for unique and interesting contributions. They have a lot of space to fill, and are constantly working to meet deadlines. If you have a product or service that could be of interest to a large segment of the population, and you can present it in an interesting, professional manner, you'll actually be doing the editors a favor.

Writing a Successful News Release

The easiest way to get a feel for the appropriate style and content of a news release is to study informational articles in newspapers and magazines. A news release must have a different tone than an advertisement. A news release should contain *news*, written in an interesting and informative style. Don't use company logos, brand names in all upper-case letters, trademark symbols, or other obvious advertising red flags. Such phrases as "major credit cards accepted" and "on sale now" are too commercial.

Stick to the "five W's": who, what, when, where, and why. Write the way you speak—in a conversational style, with perhaps a dash of humor. Editors and news directors receive an avalanche of news releases, but only the most interesting and informative get published.

The standard format for a news release is double-spaced on letter-size paper. Keep sentences to the point—no more than twenty-three words each. When communicating a thought, less is more. Never use a five-dollar word when a more common one will do. Once you've written the text, go back and circle repeated words, then replace them with fresher words. Don't leave extra spaces between paragraphs; double-space like the rest of the text. Don't use capital letters for emphasis. Keep commas and periods inside quotation marks.

Photos and graphics will make your news release more appealing, but they must be top quality. Send *original* black-and-white photos, not copies. Color prints are acceptable, but only if they are bright and in sharp focus.

You may wonder if your ordering information will be included in an article. It probably will be, for two reasons. First, it's part of the editor's responsibility to provide complete information pertaining to a story. Second, it's more convenient for the reporter to include it than to deal with a deluge of inquiries. Be casual when inserting this information in your press release, however. Avoid using such advertising jargon as "available for a limited time only for the low price of . . . " Just slide it matter-of-factly into the body of the release: "In the new book, *How to Brew Your Own Beer* ($19.95 from ABC Publishing, P.O. Box 123, San Diego, CA 33179), you'll discover the secrets of master brewers."

LEAD TIME

Lead time is the amount of time between receipt and publication of your material. Lead time for newspapers, radio, and TV is typically two weeks. However, editorial lead time for magazines can be four to eight months, so time your mailings accordingly.

GET STARTED IN YOUR OWN BACK YARD

Send your news release to one or two of your local newspapers. They're always looking for stories with homespun appeal. Remember, the goal is to attract curiosity and interest that translate into orders. A few weeks after you hit the papers, send your release to local radio and TV stations. They have shows that regularly feature local guests.

While I primarily focus on print media in this section, the process for sending broadcast media releases is similar, with a few subtle differences. The broadcasters aren't as concerned with journalistic style and format, as long as the information is concise and of interest to their audience. If your subject is unique, unusual or compelling enough, you may get a call from a producer asking you to appear as a guest. But we'll explore broadcast media more thoroughly later in this chapter.

Be sure to address your news release to a specific person, including his or her title. After you've sent out your releases, don't just sit back and wait for the results. Follow up. Make phone calls to be sure they were received. A little politeness and humility can go a long way. Don't forget to follow up by sending another package three or four months later. Some reviewers may have missed your first release, or may have heard about you in the interim.

Online Media Searches

One of the best ways to find the names of specific reporters who cover your field is through an online search. By doing a

---

POWERTIP

The "double exposure" newspaper publicity method. Send a news release to your local paper offering your services as a guest expert in your field, and invite readers to call you with their questions. Make sure your phone number and hours of availability are highlighted. Then invite the reporter to follow up with a second story featuring the most commonly asked questions, along with your advice. Not only do you control the results, you also receive a double blast of free publicity that firmly establishes you as an expert in your field.

keyword search, you can find writers who may be interested in your story, and obtain copies of their previous articles in order to get a feel for content and style. For example, if you're promoting a line of novelty T-shirts, you would search for articles containing the word "T-shirts." For information about online searches contact:

> Dialog: (800) 334-2564
> Dow Jones News/Retrieval: (800) 522-3567
> LEXIS-NEXIS: (800) 227-4908

Submit a Camera-Ready Article to Weekly Newspapers Across the Country

There are more than 7,000 small-market shopping newspapers and weeklies nationwide. Although they usually have circulation under 30,000, some of these publications have very loyal readers. These papers have skeleton writing staffs and will sometimes print one- or two-column, camera-ready articles submitted by freelance writers. So instead of preparing a news release for these publications work from, you can actually write your own article for publishing. Human interest stories are the most popular with editors, who prefer articles of one or two columns in length. Follow examples from your local newspaper.

In the main body of the article, remember to stick to the five W's: who, what, when, why, where. At the end of the article, include an address or telephone number where interested readers can contact you for more information.

POWERTIP

Ask for endorsements. This is your ticket to additional publicity. Provide an endorsement you would like a reviewer to use about your product, and when he or she agrees, you can use the endorsement for future publicity. Simply write a blurb illustrating a particular strength of your product, and ask the reviewer to change it any way they like. It's easier for them to revise than create. Example: "Joe Black gives you the facts without the hype." —Betsy Sullivan, producer, Rick Dees Show, KIIS-FM, Los Angeles.

Bradley Communications offers a mailing list of more than 2,000 weeklies that have been known to use this type of article. For information call (800) 989-1400, ext. 415.

How to Get Your Product Mentioned in Trade Publications

In this section, we're going to focus on trade publications that specialize in your specific business. There are over 60,000 such magazines and newsletters, covering virtually every subject you can think of. The following is a successful system that will expose your product not only to prospective customers, but to your entire industry. This can lead to valuable contacts and increased marketing possibilities.

The first step is to obtain a sample issue of each publication (see the list of resources at the end of this chapter). You will find each publication's contact information on its *masthead*, or credit box, on the second or third page of every issue. Call the advertising department and ask for a media kit. This will include circulation and qualitative data, advertising rates, and a copy of a recent or upcoming issue.

Check out the "new product" sections of the publications to get a feel for the kind of products covered and the format and style used. Grab a note pad or tape recorder and make some notes so that you can tailor your submission accordingly. Limit your release to one or two pages, and downplay the sales hype. Communicate the features and benefits of your product, and highlight the comparisons to similar existing products. Make sure the information is credible and reliable.

Now, aim your piece toward the "new products" or "what's new" sections of the publications. These high-profile areas are read by more prospective customers, manufacturers, and other potential strategic contacts than any other area of the magazine. While some magazines charge a fee for new product listings, most do not; it's their job to report news of interest to their readers. Go with the free listings.

Include a 5 by 7-inch, glossy black-and-white photo of your product. You can have this done by a professional photographer for as little as forty dollars. This may get you some extra space in the publication and draw increased attention to your item. Be creative. Come up with an angle or hook to make the photo compelling. The most interesting photos sometimes end up on the cover!

Some magazines also require a product sample. Include test results, testimonials, and other supporting documentation, and don't forget to include a short letter of introduction.

Your completed package should include the following:

- Cover letter and news release on your business letterhead.
- Photo of your product (protected with a piece of cardboard) with business card attached.
- Reprints of prior reviews and other supporting documents.
- Folder-sized envelopes (9 by 12-inch or larger if needed).

Next, make a list of at least forty magazines. You need at least that many to achieve optimum coverage. Divide them into two lists. The first is your "A" list, and should be made up of the top eight publications specifically geared to your target market. The remaining thirty-two publications should include related trade and consumer magazines. Wherever possible, get the name of the appropriate recipient for your package. Otherwise, address it in care of the "News Release Department."

Now you're ready to launch your mailing. For even distribution and maximum exposure, follow the strategic schedule below:

> **List 1:** From your base of forty trade magazines and consumer publications, choose two from your A list, and twelve from your B list. These fourteen will be the first publications to receive your packages.
> **List 2:** Select another twelve magazines, including two more from your A list.
> **List 3:** Group the remaining sixteen magazines, including the final four from your A list.

Begin by mailing your packages to List 1 only. Regular postage is fine, but if you can afford to ship overnight or by certified mail your release will command prompt attention. Your product announcements from List 1 should begin appearing in print within approximately sixty days.

Send packages to List 2 approximately five weeks after your mailing to List 1. Five weeks after that, launch List 3. Keep several packages as a backup in case an original gets misplaced by a magazine, or in case you discover additional publications to send them to.

Don't forget to follow up. This is a crucial step in the process. About ten days after each mailing, call the magazines and ask for the editorial department. Confirm receipt of your release, and ask when it will be published. If you get a negative response, don't panic; you're not through yet. Call again and ask to speak to the general sales manager. Be friendly, and inform the manager of your marketing plans. Suggest that a few inches of space in their magazine might lead to a future advertising alliance between your companies. Never have this conversation with an editor or a reporter. You will probably insult them, and your release will probably end up filed under "G."

Electronic News Releases

Electronic news releases are sent to publications via the Internet or a wire service and fed directly into editorial computers, where they often receive attention more quickly than a hard copy. An electronic release may remain in a database for years. LEXIS-NEXIS has releases dating back as far as 1980.

Following are two firms that specialize in writing and submitting news releases:

Twin Peaks Press: (800) 637-2256

For a flat fee of $795, Twin Peaks Press will prepare a 400-word news release for you and send it over the wire service to more than 2,300 editors, news directors, and producers across the country.

PR Newswire
150 East 58th Street, 31st Floor
New York, NY 10155
(800) 334-6692

PR Newswire distributes news releases to the national media or to specific contacts. An annual membership costs $75 plus an additional charge per release. You can also send your own news releases electronically over PR Newswire's *US1* for $465 for the first 400 words.

15,000 Opportunities for Free Publicity

Publicity Blitz from Bradley Communications is an excellent source of key contacts, including more than 15,000 magazines, newspapers, news syndicates, columnists, and radio/TV/cable programs. If you're serious about generating free publicity, this may be the only source you'll need. Listings are divided into convenient subject categories, and are updated quarterly. The data include names, titles, addresses, phone numbers, and fax numbers, provided on either PC or Macintosh diskette. If you don't have a computer, printouts are available. Here's what *Publicity Blitz* includes:

DAILY NEWSPAPER EDITORS

Lists almost 1,300 dailies including such large-market newspapers as *The Wall Street Journal, USA Today, New York Times,* and *Washington Post.* Mail your news release to all of them or target by city, state, market rank, or circulation size. Editors, reporters, and columnists are listed by name and indexed by twenty-six different topics.

SYNDICATED COLUMNISTS

Nationally syndicated columns and columnists are listed, from Ann Landers to *Your Taxes,* searchable by the same subject codes as magazines and newsletters. If just one of these writers mentions you, you could get exposure to hundreds of newspapers across the country and internationally!

MAGAZINES AND NEWSLETTER EDITORS

Includes editors at domestic offices for the Associated Press, UPI, Reuters, Gannett News, and other news services. Names of over 2,800 consumer and trade publications, ranging from national magazines such as *Time, Newsweek, Forbes, Good Housekeeping, Parade,* and *Smart Money* to local publications such as *Detroit Parent,* and specialized newsletters such as *Telephone Selling Report.* Also listed are the subject(s) each company and person covers, circulation, geographic coverage, which magazines review books (and the book editor's name), and which publications mention products (and the product editor's name).

BROADCAST MEDIA CONTACTS

More than 1,200 contacts at news/talk and music radio stations are listed, as well as the top fifty national cable and TV talk shows. Includes local radio shows and national programs such as *Today, Good Morning America, Rikki Lake,* and *The Late Show with David Letterman,* some of whom pay travel expenses for their guests.

AND MORE!

The folks at Bradley really did their homework. In addition to the database, they will send you the following booklets: *Print Publicity Secrets, Guide to Major Book Reviewers, Top National TV Talk Shows,* and *Talk Show Publicity Secrets.* Publicity Blitz costs about $300, and is worth its weight in gold. For information or to order contact:

> **Bradley Media Publications**
> 135 East Plumstead Avenue, P.O. Box 1206
> Lansdowne, PA 19050-8206
> (800) 989-1400
> Fax: (610) 284-4704

POWERTIP

Get your product featured on TV game shows. To receive an information kit, write: Game Show Placements, 7011 Willoughby Avenue, Hollywood, CA 90038.

One-Stop Shopping for Publicity Seekers

News USA is a company that syndicates features, news, and information to virtually every newspaper, radio, and television station in the U.S. Their slogan is "nationwide coverage, guaranteed." You provide the basic information about your organization and concepts, and their professional journalists will prepare a camera-ready feature story including a photo or graphic. All copy is cleared with you prior to distribution and rewrites are free. They'll even send you a free prototype, along with distribution and cost projections, at no obligation.

Camera-ready news features and columns are disseminated bi-weekly to 10,000 newspapers over the Internet, in printed tabloid format, or on computer disks. You will receive actual newspaper clippings, signed broadcast usage statements, and air checks (recorded copies) with monthly reports. News USA can also broadcast-fax your news release to many radio stations simultaneously—an effective way of getting interview bookings. They cover not only English-language media, but also all 610 Spanish-language media nationwide, reaching the twenty-five-million-plus Hispanic population.

Fees include everything from creative work to media distribution. If you want to tell the world about your new product or service, establish yourself as an expert in your field, or even start your own newspaper column, contact:

News USA
8300 Boone Boulevard, #810
Vienna, VA 22182
(703) 827-5800
(800) 355-9500
On the Web: *http://www.newsusa.com*

Become an Official Expert in Your Field

The Yearbook of Experts, Authorities, and Spokespersons is circulated free to 14,000 TV and radio stations, magazines, and daily newspapers in North America. You can buy a reference listing (approximately one-sixth of a page) for about $375. A full-page ad costs about $1,200. This widespread visibility is the equivalent of sending out *four mailbags* of news releases. For information contact:

Broadcast Interview Source
2233 Wisconsin Avenue NW
Washington, D.C. 20007
(202) 333-4904
On the Web: *http://www.yearbook.com*

Appear on Radio and TV Talk Shows

There are more than 10,000 guests appearing on some 4,500 local interview and talk shows across the country, and 94 percent of them are *not* famous people. This is the kind of exposure and advertising you couldn't buy—and it's free. An appearance on the *Today* show can sell 3,000 copies of a book, while an author who appeared on *Donahue* sold 50,000! *The Radio-TV Interview Report* by Bradley Media Publications is a primary resource used by talk show producers and hosts, from AM radio to daytime TV. For about $400, they will write and place a half-page ad that reaches more than 8,000 talk show producers and hosts.

All you need is an inbound toll-free number and a news release with some background information. Put together an informative and entertaining presentation to promote your book or product, and your phone will soon be ringing off the hook with interview requests. Simply mention your toll-free number during each interview, and you could be

POWERTIP

Don't forget to tape your TV appearances. Not only will they help you get on other shows, they also make excellent promotional videos, fair, and trade show attention-getters, and potential infomercial clips. Just set your VCR, or ask a friend to tape the show for you. You can also buy a copy from services that tape everything on the air. Just give them the name of the show and the air date. Contact Radio & TV Reports, at (212) 309-1400, or Video Monitoring Services of America, at (213) 380-5011.

overwhelmed by the response. Call or write for current advertising rates and a sample copy to Bradley Media Publications (see page 104).

Build on Your Success

Publicity begets publicity; it's a snowball effect. Start with local media and use this coverage to hit regional media, all the way up to national. Whenever you do an interview that goes particularly well, ask the reporter for an endorsement that says what a terrific guest you are. Include this in future mailings. Always save your clippings and tape everything. Strategically using your publicity to get more publicity is like fueling the fire!

Cross-promote at every opportunity. If you're going to be on a local radio show, call the newspaper and let them know, and vice versa. Some other ideas:

- Announce an award. The designer Mr. Blackwell owes his career to the free publicity generated by his annual "Worst-Dressed List."
- Create your own holiday that relates to your field. The annual *Chase Calendar of Events* was practically written by publicity hounds.
- Come up with a contest or event that ties in with a local fair or convention.
- Write a letter to the editor of your local newspaper.

There's an inexhaustible supply of free publicity out there. Focus on what works best for you, and go get it!

If bright lights and microphones make you cringe, you can remain behind the scenes and still boost your credibility. However, promoting yourself and your product can be an exhilarating experience. You may discover talents you never knew you had. Publicity is like anything else; practice fosters confidence. Motivate yourself with the knowledge that you have something of value to offer. Make notes of key points, interact with callers, or audience members and have fun. As you gain experience and confidence, you'll discover that your story practically tells itself!

CHAPTER 10

FINANCING AND VENTURE CAPITAL ANGELS: ATTRACTING EAGER INVESTORS

> *When you persuade, speak of interest,*
> *not of reason.*
>
> **Benjamin Franklin**

IF YOU NEED a cash infusion to jump-start your business and have had no luck with the bank or family and friends, don't be discouraged. There are plenty of successful entrepreneurs who are eager to give something back to the system that made them wealthy. In the United States, over a quarter of a million such individual venture capitalists invest a total of ten billion dollars annually, compared to the average four billion invested by venture capital companies.

Venture capital is money invested in a business in exchange for partial ownership. Most business investments by individuals are directed toward start-up financing, whereas venture capital companies prefer to invest in established operations or new businesses with growth potential in the millions of dollars. Individual venture capitalists usually invest in groups, with a single investor averaging as much as

$50,000. Most prefer to be in and out of a deal within two to four years. They offer experience and expertise in addition to cash, and are much more supportive of potential new businesses than are lending institutions.

How to Find Investors

Finding investors can be tricky. It's best to go after more informal lenders, or "angels," than after venture capital companies. Be sure to specify these kinds of investors when making inquiries to venture capital organizations (see the Resource Directory for organizations to contact). For obvious reasons, these angels are elusive, and they operate in virtual anonymity. They don't advertise their existence. This allows them to separate the serious entrepreneur from crackpots and dabblers. You'll need a compelling, well-thought-out approach just to get to first base. In this chapter, you'll learn how to find these affluent individuals and approach them with a winning proposal.

These benefactors are not charities; they expect to make a profit on their investment. Venture capital angels didn't get where they are by being careless with money. Their piece of the action generally involves a limited partnership, or a percentage of the company via stock options if you are incorporated.

Some contracts between entrepreneurs and venture capitalists include the stipulation that no individual shall assume control of the company, but you should take the necessary precautions to maintain majority control of your business. If you're incorporated, this means retaining no less than 51 percent of the stock. Naturally, investors will expect to have a certain amount of input, but you should be responsible for the day-to-day operation of your business. If you earn the confidence of your investors, they'll probably allow you the latitude to conduct business with minimal interference.

Bear in mind that venture capitalists are generally creative, "lateral" thinkers who enjoy interacting with their

POWERTIP

To locate private investors on the Internet, visit Venture Connect's Web site, at *http://www.texel.com.*

contemporaries. Therefore, your personality and attitude are as important as your game plan, if not more so. If you're unique and creative in your presentation, you'll surely stand out among the other businesses they're considering.

In the Resource Directory at the end of this book is a list of venture capital organizations that have access to private investors. They are the buffer between entrepreneurs and investors. Their job is to review your proposal and connect you with the right people. Call them for instructions and an application. Focus on investors who are based close to the location of your business, since geographical proximity is a prime consideration.

Next, you'll need to prepare your letter of introduction and an investor prospectus. Keep the letter brief and to the point. Simply state your desire to invite private-sector investors to participate in your dynamic new venture, and stress the availability of stock options if you're incorporated. Include your telephone number, and invite them to call for additional information. Remember, the first impression you make is crucial. The letter should be printed on your company letterhead using a good typewriter or laser printer.

Your investor prospectus must provide a detailed breakdown of your business plan, including start-up costs, operating expenses, market research showing a demand for your product, and a realistic profit prognosis. A trip to your local business retailer for spreadsheets, software, or even a how-to book on the subject will help you put it all together.

The bucks for your brainchild are certainly available if you're aggressive and have a solid presentation. The venture capital angel can be your best friend in business. In addition to financing, they'll provide invaluable insight and guidance to help you along. After all, they were once in your shoes—with nothing but a dream, a desire, and a plan of action.

POWERTIP

For comprehensive materials and information about raising venture capital and locating the major players, contact:

David Silver
The Silver Press
524 Camino Del Monte Sol
Santa Fe, NM 87501
(505) 983-1769

Locate Millions in Financing in Five Minutes or Less

DataMerge, Inc., in Denver, Colorado, provides excellent databases that allow you to access thousands of active lenders, equity investors, venture capital companies, and private investors quickly and efficiently. The databases listed below are available in IBM/DOS-compatible software, in a menu-driven question-and-answer format that eliminates the guesswork of locating financing for your business.

Each database comes with a helpful glossary of finance terms and free technical support, and even software that shows you how to put together a practical, comprehensive financing proposal that gets results. You'll find listings of active firms and private individuals all over the country who have capital to lend, so you don't need to travel. Detailed profiles reveal each lender's requirements and availability:

- Specific contact names
- How much capital they can offer
- What kinds of deals they're interested in
- What they'll expect in return for financing
- Exactly what documents you need to provide

DataMerge offers two basic versions:

Professional Version (approximately $499): Contains 10,000 financing sources, including private investors, debt and equity investors, and real estate sources. It's worth the price just for the database of private individuals looking to finance unique entrepreneurial ventures.
Entrepreneur Version (approximately $139): Twenty-five hundred lenders, equity investors, and venture capital companies specializing in small-business financing.

POWERTIP

The U.S. Small Business Administration (SBA) can help you find community-based, nonprofit lenders for amounts under $10,000. If you have a great idea and a solid business plan, your credit history and collateral are of secondary concern. To find the SBA office nearest you, call (800) 827-5722 or fax (202) 205-7064 or visit their Web site at *http://www.sbaonline.sba.gov.*

For a complete information package, contact:

DataMerge, Inc.
4521 East Virginia Avenue, Suite 201
Denver, CO 80222
(303) 320-8361
(800) 580-1188

Your Financing Proposal

The first and most important step in the preparation of your comprehensive business plan is the *executive summary*, a synopsis of your business plan. It is the cornerstone on which you'll build your detailed financing proposal. While there's a wide range of information available on how to develop a business plan, much of it fails to adequately address the basic concerns of venture capitalists. If you don't have enough information to complete your executive summary, get the help of a professional to acquire the necessary information before proceeding. Your executive summary should address the following questions:

1. **How much capital do you need?** To investors, under-funding your project is an unforgivable sin. Request sufficient capital to keep the business afloat until it begins to show positive cash flow (profit after expenses). It's better to estimate high than to run short and have to raise additional capital in the midst of operations. For larger projects, consider raising capital in stages. For example, Stage One would include research and development; Stage Two would involve start-up capital, and so on.
2. **How will the money be spent?** A practical, realistic financial proposal is crucial. This is determined by your prior

experience in the business, or by comparing existing businesses in the marketplace. You can minimize the guesswork by obtaining the help of an accountant to calculate expenses. Bringing an officer of a similar business on board will go a long way toward establishing credibility and trust in the minds of potential investors.

3. **Who will be in charge of business operations?** Obviously, the larger your personal financial stake, the more comfortable investors will feel about getting involved. If you will not be in charge yourself, then someone with expertise is the best alternative.

4. **What are the projected profits of the business?** The two key words here are *generosity* and *detail* in spelling out returns for the investor. Be specific. Break returns down by month for the first year, then quarterly for the second through fifth years. Include a summary of projections that a potential investor can evaluate at a glance. Many investors expect a ten-fold return over five years.

Government Grants

Uncle Sam is not in the habit of financing just any business. Grant money almost always goes to one of two types of business: companies that have developed or are capable of developing a product or service that the government needs, or companies that will offer a service of benefit to the public at large.

The Federal Register is published each business day by the U.S. government, and carries announcements of available grants. A subscription costs $195, or you can find it at the library.

Another good publication about federal grants is the *Catalog of Federal Domestic Assistance* (CFDA), available at large public and college libraries. For information contact:

Catalog of Federal Domestic Assistance
General Services Administration
300 Seventh Street SW
Washington, DC 20407
(202) 708-5082

POWERTIP

Get a free, thorough business plan from local colleges or universities. MBA and business classes are always looking for models to work on, and may construct and evaluate your marketing plan for free. To locate colleges with these programs, contact the Small Business Advancement Center at (501) 450-5300.

Incubators

Incubators are set up by nonprofit organizations to help new businesses get off the ground by providing business and financial advice, and affordable secretarial and computer services, and sometimes office space. For information (or for a copy of the excellent book, *National Census of Seed Capital Funds*, by Richard T. Meyer, Timothy Falvey, and Min Lee) contact:

National Business Incubation Association
One President Street
Athens, OH 45701
(614) 593-4331

Incubators Times is a quarterly newsletter published by the SBA. For information contact:

Office of Private Initiatives
Small Business Administration
409 Third Street SW
Washington, DC 20416
(202) 653-7880

Various state and regional small business development organizations can help you locate concerns that make loans to small businesses. Contact:

Association of Small Business Development Centers
1313 Farnham, Suite 132
Omaha, NE 68182
(402) 595-2387

POWERTIP

One-stop financing assistance: The National Business Association is a nonprofit organization that offers special product and service discounts to small-business owners. They can also help to evaluate your chances of getting a loan before you apply for one. Call them at (800) 456-0440 and ask for a copy of *First Step Review*. They also offer three informative computer programs on writing a business plan, analyzing cash flow, and understanding profit-and-loss projections, at a cost of five dollars each. Specify your operating system when ordering the disks.

PART THREE

Million-Dollar Home-Based Businesses

CHAPTER 11

SELF-PUBLISHING: UNLIMITED WEALTH IN THE INFORMATION AGE

There are a lot more people who got rich selling cookbooks than running restaurants.

Joe Karbo

THERE MAY BE no faster, easier way for the average person to achieve financial independence than by becoming an "infopreneur." Proprietary information such as books, newsletters, reports, and audio- and videotapes, are an eight-billion-dollar industry—easily surpassing goods and services, and twice as big as the personal computer market. This amounts to 50 percent of the gross national product of the United States.

In the information age, people are hungry for "how-to" information and are willing to pay for it. If you've been putting off starting a home-based business for lack of a product, you're going to find out how easy it is to manufacture one out of paper and ink, and turn your individual expertise, interests, and hobbies into cash.

There is a potential market of more than 100 million people for informative products that can be sold by mail or-

119

der, magazines, newspapers, radio, television, and the Internet. Information is cheap and easy to produce, with minimal overhead, and brings a maximum return on your investment.

People are selling twenty-page how-to booklets for between five and twenty-five dollars each. The profit potential is simply stunning. Charles Moritz, president of Dun & Bradstreet, says, "I believe that the information industry will be the most dynamic and exciting sector of the U.S. economy, with tremendous opportunities for all."

So, what to publish? Here are a few sample how-to titles to get your imagination flowing:

> How to Get Rich in Real Estate
> How to Have a Winning Personality
> How to Run a Successful Business
> How to Lose Weight
> How to Make Your Marriage Last
> How to Marry a Millionaire
> How to Brew Your Own Beer
> How to Program Your VCR
> How to Interpret Dreams
> How to Make Doll Clothes
> How to Sell Anything
> How to Live on Five Dollars a Day

What Should You Sell?

> *A good test of the worth of a book is the number of times we can read it with profit.*
>
> **Dan Poynter**

Most people are completely intimidated at the thought of writing a book. Believe me, it doesn't take a genius to do it. Even if you have trouble writing a letter, you can write a book. If you can speak into a tape recorder, you can be an author. Many successful authors, including Dr. Ruth Westheimer, dictate their books.

The most obvious topic for a how-to book, newsletter, or audio tape is something you're already familiar with. Your individual knowledge, expertise, and hobbies can earn you more than a comfortable living. If you need inspiration, just check out the classified and display ads in magazines and supermarket tabloids. Notice the type of information that is being offered for sale. Pay particular attention to the larger ads, especially the quarter-page to full-page ads. They are obviously making money, since ads of this size are expensive to run every month. Once you realize that it isn't necessary to reinvent the wheel, you'll understand the incredible potential of marketing how-to information.

When considering subject matter, ask yourself the following questions:

- Have I determined through research that my subject is of interest to a large enough segment of the population to be successful?
- Can I provide enough reliable information on the subject to cover it thoroughly and uniquely?
- Is the subject easy to research, write about, and produce a book or booklet about?
- Will I be able to sell the completed product for at least three to four times the cost of production?

Gathering Information for Your Book

Two of the best sources of information are related trade publications and library reference books, including encyclopedias. Assemble all the information you can, focusing on new and innovative developments in the field. Be thorough and document your subject completely. You'll quickly build a sizable stack of notes. Keep them neat and handy.

If you feel a bout of procrastination coming on, remind yourself that just one successful how-to book can earn anywhere from $20,000 to $200,000 or more. Compiling the information is the toughest part of the job. As the pieces of the puzzle start coming together, it won't be long before you experience the indescribable joy and satisfaction of the birth of your "baby."

LEXIS-NEXIS

LEXIS-NEXIS is the world's largest premium information service providing legal, news, and financial information to virtually every Fortune 500 company and major law firm in the United States. LEXIS-NEXIS is also becoming a primary information provider for the international information consumer.

Currently the only way to access full LEXIS-NEXIS services on the Internet is via telnet, and this service is available to current subscribers only. If you would like to subscribe to LEXIS-NEXIS and are not certain which link below is appropriate, call their new sales office at (800) 227-4908 or (937) 865-6800, ext. 5858.

LEXIS-NEXIS also offers products and services to smaller businesses and individuals who have specific research needs. To obtain information about these services, call NEXIS Express (for business or financial information needs) or LEXIS Express (for legal information needs) at (800) 843-6476 or (937) 865-6800, ext. 5505. These research solutions can be billed to your credit card, even if you are not a current subscriber to the full LEXIS-NEXIS service offerings.

For more information, contact:

LEXIS-NEXIS
Mead Data Central
P.O. Box 933
Dayton, OH 45401
(513) 865-6800

The Outline

When it's time to put together your manuscript, gather your notes. Then assemble between six and twelve separate sheets of standard writing paper. Each sheet represents a chapter of your book, this will help you to efficiently organize the information in your notes. The average book contains six to twelve chapters, depending on the subject matter.

Take some time to think about how to organize your chapter topics and decide what your chapters will be. Number each chapter in order, making sure the information flows naturally. Then organize your notes into these chapters and establish an outline for each chapter by writing down each subject or sub-heading in point form on the appropriate chapter page.

Now tack the chapter pages in numerical order onto the wall of your office or work area. Get a cassette recorder or dictaphone and expound on all the information in your notes chapter by chapter, subheading by subheading. This will be surprisingly easy if you've read and completely grasped the information in your notes. Use as many or as few chapters as you need in order to fully explain the subject. When you've completed all the chapters, you have your book! It's inside your tape recorder, all ready to be transcribed into a manuscript.

The Manuscript

You can transcribe the manuscript yourself, ask a friend to help, or hire a college student or secretary to transfer your audio onto paper or computer disk. The completed manuscript must be proofread for structure, grammar, spelling, and punctuation. Smooth out any rough spots and rewrite where necessary. If proofreading is beyond your abilities or interest, you shouldn't have any trouble finding someone to help. Now you are ready to publish.

Publishing Your Book

Check the Resource Directory to find the help you'll need to typeset and print your manuscript. There can be a substantial difference in services and fees, so be sure to obtain several quotes in order to get the best deal. A printer will typeset and lay out your "proof," or master copy, of the book. A desktop publisher can transcribe your text onto a floppy disk. The least expensive way to print your book is by offset printing. If you will be using illustrations or graphs, you can insert these into the proofs, and make any changes to the format before you are billed for the finished package.

Upon completion, you may decide that your book isn't as thick as you would like. Here are a few tips you can use to increase its volume:

- Use enlarged margins
- Use double-spaced lines
- Print on bulk (thicker) paper
- Add illustrations, charts, and graphs

If you're computer-literate, most (if not all) of these techniques will appear outdated or even archaic. There are many excellent software programs available that make publishing child's play. However, my purpose is to demonstrate that anyone can publish a book, regardless of their resources or budget.

For the computer-literate, there is a wealth of do-it-yourself desktop publishing resources on the Web, at *http:// www.desktoppublishing.com.* Resources are constantly updated and added to ensure you get the latest cutting edge information on desktop publishing and related newsgroups and mailing lists, as well as tips on software programs such as PageMaker, Photoshop, QuarkXPress, Corel Draw, and others. This is one of the best sites of its kind on the Web.

A Word About The Kitchen Table Millionaire

How do I know self-publishing is a viable source of wealth? The book you are holding in your hands is proof. I self-published the initial version of *The Kitchen Table Millionaire* before reaching an agreement with Prima Publishing, one of the fastest growing publishing houses in North America. I had a local artist design the cover and found a manufacturer in Utah to print the books, along with six audiocassettes (I recorded the master tapes at a radio station where I was working at the time). Everything was packaged in an attractive vinyl album, and cost me about $10 per unit—which I sold for $59.95 via radio interviews and a few print advertisements in income opportunity magazines.

POWERTIP

Ask your printer for overruns of your book cover. Paste them on the front of your press kit folders for a sharp, professional look. They also look great framed on your office wall, or you can frame them and give them as gifts.

While the book-and-tapes package sold well, I knew I'd need help in order to expose the book to a wider market. I sent review copies to influential leaders in the field such as Brian Tracy, the renowned motivational expert and author, and Carolyn Tice, executive editor of *Home Business News* for the American Home Business Association. Their testimonials, along with several favorable reviews in entrepreneurial trade publications, helped me put together a dynamic proposal that caught the attention of Jennifer Basye Sander, a senior acquisitions editor at Prima. Self-publishing can be an excellent stepping stone to a publishing deal, since testimonials, press clippings, and sales figures go a long way toward illustrating the value and potential of a book.

Publishers Marketing Association

Since the subject of self-publishing can fill an entirely new book, I'll finish this chapter with the best resource I know: Publishers Marketing Association (PMA). Membership includes a newsletter and comprehensive resource directory packed with an abundance of information for the self-publisher, from novice to expert. This includes tips on interior and exterior layout and design, short-run printers, ISBN barcode specialists, marketing and publicity, and more. Membership rates are subject to change, so contact PMA for information:

**Publishers Marketing Association/
Audio Publishers Association**
2401 Pacific Coast Highway, #102-A
Hermosa Beach, CA 90254
(310) 372-2732
Fax: (310) 374-3342

CHAPTER 12

900 NUMBERS:
AN UNTAPPED SOURCE
OF INCOME POTENTIAL

I was seldom able to see an opportunity
until it had ceased to be one.

Mark Twain

THE USE OF 900 NUMBERS has ballooned into a five-billion-dol-
lar-a-year industry, and it's growing wildly. Since the birth of
the 900 number in 1980 (as a voter polling device for the
Reagan/Carter television debates), it has become one of the
single most powerful interactive marketing tools in America.
Some people are making tens of thousands of dollars per week
selling information and entertainment with a single 900 number. Getting started has become easier than ever. You can get
a 900 number for as little as a few hundred dollars.

900 numbers are different from toll-free numbers, in
that toll-free numbers allow a caller to place a long-distance
call at no cost to the caller. A caller who dials a 900 number
is charged a fee, either by the call or by the minute. These
charges are billed to the caller's monthly telephone bill and
the profits are forwarded to you, either directly from the
telephone carrier or through a service bureau, minus carrier charges and user fees.

The money you can make with your own 900 number is unbelievable. However, a 900 number is just an advertising medium. In order to succeed as an information provider (IP), you need two important things:

1. A product or subject on which you can provide useful, valuable information
2. A strategic marketing network to promote your 900 number (classified ads, radio or TV commercials)

We live in the information age. People need information quickly and conveniently, and nothing is more convenient than the telephone. People also love entertainment. There are thousands of 900-number ads for psychics, date lines, sex hot lines, and more. The reason you see them all over the place is because they are making money. If you have an idea that would appeal to a large segment of the public, you have the potential to make a killing. You can even buy a turnkey 900 number, advertise it, and collect your share of the profits from this exciting industry.

You can use 900 numbers to advertise your how-to book simply by recording interesting excerpts. Not only do you make money on each call, but you can also tell people how to order the book! If you have a product or service, you can offer industry tips or resources. There are no limits to the possibilities, as long as your information or entertainment provides value-for-value. No one will pay $1.95 a minute to hear weak or outdated information. This is where the industry earned a black eye in the early years. A successful 900 number is never a scam; it should be a genuine marketing tool.

Here are some services available by 900 numbers on the market today:

Astrology
Beauty Tips
Date Lines
Entertainment Updates
Health Tips
How-To Advice
Income Opportunities
Joke Lines

Lottery
Relationship Advice
Sports Picks
Trivia

When considering acquiring a 900 number, ask yourself the following questions:

- Do I want an original or existing program?
- What is the target audience for my service?
- Which service bureau should I use?
- How much can I charge per minute (or per call)?
- How can I advertise my number?
- What can I afford to spend on advertising?
- Can I write my own script, or do I need help?

Profit Analysis

I'm sure you've seen the many income-opportunity ads trumpeting the colossal earning power of 900 numbers. This isn't just hype. If you provide genuine information that a lot of people are interested in and you have the right advertising campaign, you can make an incredible amount of money. To illustrate, let's take a look at the numbers. Suppose you charge $1.99 per minute on your line, and you receive an average of one three-minute call per hour:

One three-minute call, at $1.99 per minute	= $5.97

Then subtract your costs:

Carrier Service Charge (10% per call)	= $5.37
Carrier Equipment Fee (75¢ per call)	= $4.62
Carrier Preamble Fee (12¢ per call)	= $4.50
Service Bureau Fee (11¢ per min. = 33¢/call)	= **$4.17** (profit per call)

Finally, calculate your take:

$4.17 per hour × 24 hours	=	**$100.08** per day
$100.08 × 7 days	=	**$700.56** per week
$700.56 × 4 weeks	=	**$2,802.24** per month
$2802.24 × 12 months	=	**$33,626.88 per year**

This doesn't include your advertising costs (see Chapter 4). Still, it's not bad for a single 900 line that pulls only one call per hour. Imagine getting 200, 500, or even 1,000 calls an hour! It's easy to see why some IPs are raking in $40,000 a month. Explosive stuff.

Current regulations stipulate a maximum rate of $5 per minute, and a maximum of $25 per call. If you charge that much, you'd better have Elvis, Marilyn, and Jesus on the line with you.

Thanks to the weasels who abuse this industry, 900 numbers still leave a bad taste in some people's mouths. This is why it's so important to charge a reasonable fee and provide legitimate information. You can make a very good living charging $1.99 or $2.99 per minute on a high volume of calls. Get a feel for pricing by comparing existing ads.

Service Bureaus

Because getting a 900 line directly from AT&T, Sprint, or MCI will cost about $50,000, you will probably want to work with a service bureau. For a small start-up fee and a monthly service charge, or a pre-negotiated percentage of your monthly gross, a good service bureau can be an asset to your operation.

In addition to forwarding the necessary forms, activating your 900 number, and deducting telephone company charges, service bureaus track your calls, estimate your monthly profits, and transfer your cash in half the time it would take you to get them from the telephone carrier. This is called *factoring*. Some service bureaus charge a small fee for this convenience, but it's worth it. Factoring is an important feature to ask for

POWERTIP

Standards of Practice for Voice Information Services is a free, one-page guideline concerning ethics, informational content, and advertising in the 900-number industry. Send a self-addressed, stamped envelope to:

The Information Industry Association
555 New Jersey Avenue NW, Suite 800
Washington, DC 20001

when shopping for a service bureau. Other important items to ask about include the range of service features, fees, and, of course, references.

American Audiotext publishes a quarterly newsletter for IPs. Call their demonstration line at (800) 733-7790 or call direct at (800) 432-0080. You'll also find additional information, including a list of 900-number service bureaus, in the Resource Directory.

Advertising Your 900 Number

The best way to advertise your 900 line is via magazine and newspaper classified ads (see Chapter 4). In the case of magazines, bigger publications are not always better. Focus on the ones that reach your target market. Advertise in magazines that feature several pages of classified ads on a regular basis. This indicates that the ads are getting results, or they wouldn't be running as long as they are. Call or write to magazines for their rate cards. Start with small, inexpensive ads and test, test, test until you know they're pulling well.

CHAPTER 13

AUCTIONS AND CONSIGNMENT: MAKE YOUR FORTUNE BUYING AND SELLING NATIONWIDE

Opportunity is missed by most people because it is dressed in overalls and looks like work.

Thomas Edison

WHEN IT COMES to pennies-on-the-dollar deals on virtually every item imaginable, auctions remain a well-kept secret. Why? Knowledge is power. Insiders know that the fewer bidders there are, the better the deals. Competition creates inflation. Fortunes have been and continue to be made by those who know how to use auctions to their best advantage: purchasing high-demand merchandise and big-ticket items for resale.

There are amazing deals to be found at auctions every day on furniture, appliances, electronic equipment, automobiles, recreational vehicles, aircraft, real estate, and more. The key is to know what to buy that will resell quickly at a sizable markup, and how to bid effectively without spending a lot of time and money. You can make a very comfortable living in the auction game, and the techniques are surprisingly easy.

In this chapter, you will learn about the various types of auctions, where they're held, how to bid (in person or across the country), and, most importantly, what to buy and sell for maximum profit. You make your money by acquiring merchandise at auctions and reselling to the public. The key to this system is knowing what to buy, how much to pay, and how to guarantee a profit upon resale.

The standard rule is: *Never purchase anything you cannot resell quickly, at a profit margin of at least 75 to 100 percent.*

What to Buy and Sell for Profit

The idea is to make your time and effort pay off as handsomely as possible by turning over the merchandise quickly, and reinvesting the proceeds toward even greater income. Market demand has shown some products to be more successful than others for resale. Here are some of the best items to buy and resell:

- Appliances such as refrigerators, dishwashers, microwave ovens, washers, and dryers
- Furniture such as sofas, chairs, coffee and end tables, dinette and bedroom sets, and office furniture
- Automobiles, especially economy and mid-sized cars, trucks, and sports cars

Here are the best places to advertise your merchandise when it's time to resell:

- Newspaper classified ads
- Flea markets and swap meets
- Bulletin boards in malls, community centers, and apartment buildings

Locating Auctions

With the exception of some government auctions, most can be found in the classified section of your newspaper under "Auctions," or check the Yellow Pages under "Auction Houses" and "Auctioneers." Call and tell them that you're interested in upcoming auctions. If you become friendly with these people, you may get on their mailing list and you might even receive a few inside tips on some sweet deals. With U.S. government auctions, you can usually write to the agencies and ask to be placed on their mailing lists.

GENERAL SERVICES ADMINISTRATION AUCTIONS

The General Services Administration (GSA) is the government clearing house for surplus and seized property. It is known as "The Millionaire Maker" by entrepreneurs who have cashed in on unbelievable deals on everything from residential, commercial, and industrial real estate to vehicles, motorcycles, recreational vehicles, boats, and aircraft. The Drug Enforcement Administration, FBI, and U.S. Border Patrol use it to dispose of property, and GSA listing sheets are a great way to find valuable real estate deals. The easiest way to keep informed of GSA auctions is to get on the GSA mailing lists. The federal publication *Commerce Business Daily* also carries notices of GSA auctions.

Merchandise is usually sold by competitive sealed bid. Sales are usually cash only, so you'll need to make the necessary arrangements. When bidding on real estate, a deposit of 10 percent of your bid is required. This deposit is refundable if your bid is not accepted.

You can contact the GSA at:

General Services Administration
18th and F Streets NW
Washington, DC 20405
(202) 708-5804

When you receive notice of an upcoming auction, the telephone number for the appropriate regional office will be included. Call and ask for an official sealed bidder's form; you can't participate without it. Arrange for additional cash financing if you need it. You'll find a complete list of GSA offices in the Resource Directory.

DEFENSE DEPARTMENT AUCTIONS

These auctions are generally held for the disposal of government vehicles and agricultural and mechanical equipment.

Contact your nearest Defense Reutilization and Marketing Department (listings are provided in the Resource Directory) to receive regular merchandise catalogs. Your name will be dropped from the list if you don't participate.

U.S. MARSHALS' AUCTIONS

These are auctions ordered by a federal court, and may include property seized by the IRS, FBI, or Customs Department. Items include vehicles, aircraft, boats, and jewelry. They are advertised through legal notices in newspapers and in public buildings such as courthouses. There are some unbelievable deals at Marshals' auctions. Cash or certified payment (money order, cashier's check) at the time of sale is the rule.

U.S. BORDER PATROL AUCTIONS

While your chances of finding a deal on a Ferrari, Porsche, or BMW are rare, you'll still find incredible bargains on thousands of vehicles at Border Patrol auctions. When people transport illegal aliens into the country, their vehicles are confiscated and sold at auction on a monthly basis. The deals are terrific, since this type of auction is the least known and most difficult to find. The U.S. Border Patrol operates through the GSA, with auctions held in the border states of California, New Mexico, Arizona, and Texas.

Contact the Border Patrol nearest you (see the Resource Directory), and ask to receive a program for an upcoming sale. This will tell you whether the sale will be by oral auction or "spot bid." With a spot bid, after previewing the vehicles, you fill out a card with your name, item number, and bid. The cards are passed to auction employees, who determine the highest bids. Never bid more than 50 percent of the vehicle's wholesale value. This assures you of a decent resale profit even if there are some hidden mechanical defects.

U.S. CUSTOMS AUCTIONS

People assume that the only items to be found at Customs auctions are liquor, gifts, and personal items seized from U.S. citizens traveling abroad who were nabbed at the border. However, there can be a wide variety of valuable merchandise available for literally pennies on the dollar at Customs auctions.

When Customs officials bust drug smugglers, seizure laws allow agents to confiscate not just the drugs, but also the vehicles used to transport them. This includes cars, trucks, vans, RVs, and aircraft. Hundreds of newer-model vehicles are seized every month across the U.S.

Many individuals and businesses order goods from overseas, then fail to pay the import tax and duty on arrival. This merchandise includes furniture, tools, machinery, clothing, electronic equipment, TVs, stereos, computers, liquor—the list is endless.

Due to a severe shortage of storage space for this merchandise, frequent Customs auctions are held featuring extremely low minimum bids. Registration and viewing are held in advance, and you need to bring certified funds. But beware: there are so many tremendous deals at these auctions that you'll need to keep close tabs on your budget in order to avoid going wild like a kid in a candy store!

To learn about upcoming auctions in your area, use the convenient U.S. Customs Public Auction Hotline. Using a touch-tone telephone, call (703) 351-7887 and press the appropriate number for the following services:

1   Subscriber Information
2   General Information
3   Eastern U.S. Sales Information
4   Central U.S. Sales Information
5   Western U.S. Sales Information
7   Comments and Suggestions
8   Miami, Florida Sales Center
9   Jersey City, New Jersey Sales Center
10 Specialty and Consignment Sales (Eastern U.S.)
11 El Paso, Texas Sales Center
12 Edinburg, Texas Sales Center
13 Laredo, Texas Sales Center
14 Specialty and Consignment Sales (Central U.S.)
15 Los Angeles, California Sales Center
16 San Diego, California Sales Center
17 Nogales, Arizona Sales Center
18 Specialty and Consignment Sales (Western U.S.)

IRS AUCTIONS

You know what happens when you don't pay your taxes: Uncle Sam seizes your property, and it ends up on the auction block. Since the IRS has more stuff than it knows what to do with, you'll find deals on everything under the sun. Call your district IRS office to get on its mailing list (c/o Chief of Collections Division). If you are not allowed to join a list by district, ask for a list of field offices.

Mailing lists are determined by geographic location or particular items of interest, so when you receive your bidder's application, be specific. If they think you're just a dabbler, they'll drop you from the list. Lists are updated frequently, so you need to keep reapplying. You may be required to pay a refundable deposit of 20 percent for sealed bids. Be careful to check item descriptions carefully. If you purchase seized property at an IRS auction, you may be liable for any liens against the property prior to seizure, so always obtain certification of any liabilities at the time of sale.

U.S. POSTAL SERVICE AUCTIONS

USPS auctions include anything that is lost and has been unclaimed in the mail. They are advertised in the newspaper or on post office bulletin boards. Merchandise may be sold in "lots"—large boxes full of a variety of items. Always inspect everything ahead of time.

VETERANS AFFAIRS REPOSSESSION SALES

Whether you are looking for an investment property or a home for your family, Veterans Affairs (VA) is a great source of bargains. When a veteran uses military benefits to purchase a home, the VA doesn't actually lend the money; it underwrites, or insures, the loan. If the vet defaults on the loan, the VA (or U.S. government) forecloses and assumes ownership of the property. The VA is currently in possession of approximately 20,000 vacant homes, making them a very motivated seller. You don't have to be a veteran to purchase these properties.

Call around to find a real estate broker who deals in VA repossessions. Since the VA pays a discount to real estate brokers, but not to private investors, you might as well let the broker deal with the paperwork. The VA conveniently uses a combined credit application and contract, so a broker should be able to submit your offer and get a response within a week. If your offer is accepted, the VA sets the closing date, and the deal becomes a standard real estate transaction.

Ask the broker for a VA Sales List Sheet. Read the sales terms and conditions thoroughly. Because the VA is a highly motivated seller, you'll find its terms much more favorable than those of banks. You will probably have to put a $500 deposit on your bid, refundable if your offer is rejected.

If you provide your own financing, the VA will give you a 10 percent discount, and you can also increase your chances of having your bid accepted.

DEPARTMENT OF HOUSING AND URBAN DEVELOPMENT SALES

The Department of Housing and Urban Development (HUD) is the federal agency charged with providing fair housing for Americans. HUD offers a variety of lender plans for building, purchasing, and rehabilitating all kinds of property. Although the actual loans are made by banks, they are guaranteed by the government through HUD. If the borrower defaults and the bank forecloses, HUD buys out the loan and assumes ownership. Once again, Uncle Sam becomes a motivated seller, making HUD one of the most lucrative sources for real estate deals in the country.

Sometimes HUD will perform maintenance and repairs on a property, while other property is sold as is. Just like Veterans Affairs, HUD sells property by sealed bid, and requires offers to be submitted through a real estate broker. Ask your broker for a HUD foreclosure list, or contact your local HUD office (c/o the Regional Administrator) and ask to get on its mailing list.

Bidding on HUD properties is easy and convenient, since they provide you with all the necessary forms. Your broker can answer any questions you have. Bids must include a deposit of 10 percent, refundable if rejected. The highest bid is not always the winner. An owner-occupant bid may receive preference over an investor bid. However, you can still submit a first-come, first-served backup bid on the property. If you're outbid but the sale doesn't close within forty-five days, you could still get the property.

SMALL BUSINESS ADMINISTRATION SALES

The Small Business Administration (SBA) was established by the government in the early fifties to promote small business. It routinely writes and guarantees loans to new small businesses. The failure rate of these businesses is astronomical. Once again (sigh), the government becomes a motivated seller of foreclosed business properties. If you're looking for a commercial real estate investment opportunity, the SBA has some sweet deals.

SBA foreclosure property is divided into two categories: personal property and real property. Personal property is usually sold through a private auction house. Real property can be sold by public auction, sealed bid, or negotiable sale. You'll find these sales announced in newspapers and via public postings. Contact your local auction houses to get on their mailing lists, or call your regional SBA office for a list of district offices. This is where you'll find the private auctioneers who have been contracted to conduct sales in your area.

BANKRUPTCY AUCTIONS

Here's another great source of bargains. Whenever someone declares bankruptcy, auctions are held to liquidate the petitioner's assets for distribution amongst creditors. These are usually sealed-bid auctions. Contact your local bankruptcy court (located in the local Federal Building) to get on the mailing list.

ESTATE AUCTIONS

Here's another little-known jewel in the auction game. Estate sales are the result of people "shuffling off their mortal coil" without leaving a will or beneficiaries. The dear departed's heirs, or a court, end up liquidating the personal property and/or real estate and splitting the profits. This usually involves an executor or an attorney.

Check for notices in the newspaper. If real estate is involved, the executor may hire a broker to sell the property by sealed bid. You may need to provide a deposit, submitted with a specific form provided by the broker. Contact your county office to locate these property listings. Estate sales may also be carried out through an auction house, with various articles sold together in lots.

POLICE AUCTIONS

Police auctions are known for both their bounty of merchandise and their light attendance. These auctions are held for the disposal of recovered stolen or abandoned property, such as vehicles, televisions, stereos, appliances, cameras, bicycles, and motorcycles. You'll find police auctions listed in the newspaper classifieds, or by calling your local precinct. These sales are also known for remarkably low minimum bids, since everything must go. Merchandise is sold as is, on a cash-and-carry basis.

Previewing and Bidding

Next to the actual bidding, the most important part of any auction is the previewing. When the location, date, and time are announced, you'll be advised of the previewing. Familiarize yourself with the items for sale, ask questions, look for defects, and make the necessary arrangements so that you have cash to cover your purchases. Remember, merchandise is auctioned as is, and getting a refund may be difficult, if not impossible. Make sure you know exactly what you're bidding on and how much you're willing to spend.

After you've previewed the merchandise and made your list, determine the absolute limit you will pay for each item. Write it down, and stick to it. In the excitement and frenzy of bidding, people get carried away and wind up paying much more than they intended. Remember, you need to make a profit of between 75 and 100 percent on resale.

Arrive early for the auction, and take a seat as close to the auctioneer as possible. Wear a bright-colored shirt or hat so that you stand out. Always maintain eye contact with the auctioneer during the bidding. Concentrate on the rhythm of the auctioneer's patter, and don't be afraid to ask to have a price repeated if you miss something. Stay focused.

Sometimes bidding signals can get confusing. Subtle gestures such as a tip of the hand or hat might not be enough to get the auctioneer's attention. After you've been to a few auctions and have become familiar to the auctioneers, you might develop a few signals that will give you an edge. Otherwise, a hearty wave of your bidder's card will do the trick.

It might help you to attend an auction without bidding, in order to learn the ropes and get a feel for the atmosphere.

Always hang in until the end of the auction. Remember, people will get tired, bored, and need to relieve the babysitter. Many of the best deals are made after most of the competition has gone home.

Be aware of the rules of the auction ahead of time (deposits, down payments, etc.) and make sure you have enough cash or a letter of credit from your bank. That said, relax and enjoy yourself as you make a killing as an auction entrepreneur!

Earn a Six-Figure Income as a Part-Time Auction Consignor

Of the estimated $200 billion in merchandise sold at auctions every year, a single item stands head and shoulders above the rest in both value and bidder popularity: jewelry. Nearly three-quarters of all bidders are regular jewelry buyers, and the more bidders there are, the higher the price. Even though jewelry is in premium demand, auctioneers across the country continue to pay near-retail prices.

The markup on precious jewelry from manufacturer to retailer is between 500 and 700 percent. For example, if the cost of manufacturing an item is $100, the retail price would be between $500 and $700. This represents an extraordinary opportunity in an unlimited field with minimum competition for "consignors"— entrepreneurs who routinely purchase wholesale jewelry and resell it at auctions for incredible profits.

An excellent source of consignment jewelry is The Valencia Collection, from Anka Company. This twenty-three-year-old Rhode Island–based wholesaler offers a superb selection of gold rings and jewelry, a lifetime guarantee, prompt repair service, and dealer aids. For a catalog and information kit, contact:

Anka Company
40 Freeway Drive
Cranston, RI 02920
(800) 556-7768
Fax: (401) 567-2159

Start by getting a mailing list of auctioneers across the country. You establish your network by mailing letters to 100 or more auctioneers, introducing yourself as a consignor of precious jewelry, and inviting them to call your toll-free number for a list of merchandise. You supply merchandise for auctioneers to sell by reserve bid in exchange for a 10 percent commission. That's it. You collect a check from sales within a week of the auction, and bank the cash!

The profit margins can be astounding, anywhere from 150 to 500 percent. For each dollar you invest, that's a return of between $2.50 and $6.50. After the 10 percent auctioneers' commission, your net profit is $2.25 to $5.95 for every dollar invested. Many individuals earn $100,000 to $300,000 or more per year, working only five or six hours a week—and the field is wide open!

Once you've established your network and are ready to ship the merchandise, package each item in a separate white envelope, with the following information printed on the outside: your name, date of auction, item description, and the minimum acceptable bid (your cost plus auctioneer commission and shipping charges). While getting stuck with unsold product is rare thanks to the low price, if it does happen, simply request that any unsold items be returned to you for consignment at another auction.

STEPS FOR SUCCESS

In order to succeed as an auction consignor, you should follow these steps:

1. Set up your business, bank account, letterhead, voicemail service, and toll-free number.
2. Obtain auctioneers' mailing lists.
3. Mail letters to auctioneers introducing yourself as a consignor of precious jewelry, and invite them to call you for details. You might also include a list of catalog merchandise.
4. Mail or fax your merchandise line to auctioneers. Find out when the auctions are held.
5. Ship merchandise to auctioneers by First Class mail with a return receipt, to ensure a signed record. Remember to specify reserve bid only.
6. Negotiate net payment terms with auctioneers of five to seven days after the auction takes place.
7. Reinvest. Expand your network of auctioneers, order more merchandise, and multiply your wealth!

CHAPTER 14

PAPER POWER: THE EXPLOSIVE NEW REAL ESTATE PARADIGM

People are always blaming their
circumstances for what they are.
I don't believe in circumstances.
The people who get on in this world
are the people who get up and look for
the circumstances they want, and,
if they can't find them, make them.

George Bernard Shaw

A FASCINATING NEW ERA of opportunity exists in real estate to-day. It's the buying and selling of privately held mortgages, or "paper." Billions of dollars in real estate paper changes hands in cities and towns across America on a daily basis. The chief benefit of paper, as opposed to investing in actual real estate, is expediency. When you buy paper, you don't assume ownership of the property, you own the paper that is secured by the real estate. When you purchase investment property, you also assume the headaches: property taxes, repairs, renovations, and rent collection. With paper, if a mortgagor becomes delinquent in making payments, your investment remains secure. You may foreclose and still realize a profit.

What Is Paper?

Paper is extremely flexible, and is less risky than dabbling in the stock market or investing in limited partnerships. Basically, dealing in paper involves locating and buying privately held mortgages, and quickly reselling them to real estate investors for a profit. This profit ranges from $2,500 to $25,000 per transaction, and, best of all, you can enter this lucrative field with little or no cash. All you need is a basic understanding of real estate and the methodical techniques you will learn about in this chapter.

The keys to success in paper are:

- Effectively determining the value of mortgage property (you can do this yourself or use an appraisal agency)
- Utilizing the "time value of money," meaning that cash today is worth more than it will be in the future

This is the axis upon which the paper game revolves, since it provides the powerful leverage you will use to enlighten private mortgage holders about a win-win opportunity that they probably aren't aware of. Most of these individuals collect monthly payments and interest on their property, but they don't realize that they don't have to wait the full term of the mortgage to get their cash.

Paper transactions benefit both buyer and seller. The seller receives cash in exchange for the mortgage, and the buyer then sells the mortgage to one of many active real estate investors across the country. Some real estate seminars perpetuate the myth that the only way to find these investors is through their company. I recently attended a seminar given by an outfit that offered their services as paper buyers, but only if I enrolled in their $5,000 course. Forget about expensive middlemen. Finding active real estate investors is as easy as placing a classified ad in the newspaper.

Buying and selling paper is a booming, flexible industry with a wide open playing field. Paper is a high-yield investment that offers instant cash flow, and an excellent long-term investment because of its liquidity; it provides both principal and interest. You can even hold on to some property, live on the interest, and reinvest the principal. Locating privately held mortgage property is easy, thanks to a little-known source that you'll discover later in this chapter. Paper is as close to a guaranteed investment as you'll find, because it represents secured property. By contrast, if your stock or limited partnership performs badly, you're up a creek.

Consider the following example, and notice the important role the "time value of money" plays in the process:

Helen has a single-family home on the market for $120,000. Dave is interested in the property and has a $30,000 cash down payment, but needs to finance the other $90,000. Instead of going to the bank for a loan, Dave asks Helen if she'll agree to take the $30,000 in cash and hold a $90,000 mortgage for the rest.

Helen would in effect be lending Dave $90,000. The moment Helen agrees, paper is created. It's a win-win deal. Dave benefits because he can close the deal faster and with less red tape than if he had gone to a bank or credit union. Helen agrees to accept 11 percent interest with no fees or points on the loan, and she does her own credit check. Helen wins, because had Dave secured a bank loan and paid her the full amount in cash, she would automatically be hit with a sizable capital gains tax and other penalties. If she put the cash into a standard interest-bearing account, she'd earn only 5 or 6 percent interest. By holding the mortgage herself, she receives 11 percent, plus prenegotiated payments of $900 every month from Dave for the next 360 months. Most importantly, Helen stands to make three times the original $90,000 over the entire thirty-year term of the mortgage.

So Helen gets $30,000 in cash and a $90,000 mortgage from Dave for a total of $120,000. Dave assumes ownership of the property, with Helen holding a promissory note for $90,000. This kind of deal occurs every day across the country, resulting in billions of dollars in real estate paper.

Let's fast-forward one year. Dave has made twelve payments of $900 each month. Helen wants to cash out, and is looking to sell the approximate balance of $89,700 on Dave's note. She sees an ad in the real estate classifieds that simply states:

"Will Pay Cash for Your Mortgage. Call Jim: 555-1234."

Helen contacts Jim and tells him about the house she sold to Dave a year ago, taking back a $90,000 mortgage with monthly payments of $900 over thirty years. The balance is currently $89,700. She asks Jim if he would be interested in buying the mortgage for $89,700 in cash. Jim declines. Helen is perplexed until Jim explains that, since he'd be receiving his money over the next twenty-nine years, the dollar value will depreciate because of inflation, recession, and so on. Therefore, if Jim is to pay cash today in exchange for cash tomorrow, it is reasonable to expect a discount. The longer you wait to collect, the higher the discount. The shorter the wait, the lower the discount.

Jim offers Helen $60,000 for the $89,700 mortgage. Helen agrees to the discount so that she can get her cash in a lump sum. The preliminary paperwork is completed, and Jim signs an option giving him forty-five days to close the deal. Unless Jim has the $60,000 in cash, he now has forty-five days to find a buyer willing to pay more than $60,000 for Helen's property. The difference will be Jim's profit. Jim searches the classified ads for real estate investors, and also takes out an ad of his own that reads: "Mortgage for Sale. Call Jim: 555-1234."

Jim gets a call from a real estate investor named Bob. Jim tells Bob that he has a note for $89,700 with monthly payments of $900, and twenty-nine years remaining. Bob asks a few questions about the location and condition of the property, the overall market, and the tenant's payment record. After conducting an appraisal, Bob makes Jim an offer of $70,000 for the note. This figure accurately reflects the time value of money.

Now all Jim has to do is put the deal to bed, and he makes a cool $10,000. Not bad for a couple of classified ads, a little research, and a few phone calls. This type of deal was once the exclusive domain of bankers and wealthy financiers. Now they are made in the private sector with people just like Helen, Jim, and Bob.

Jim now has two ways to close the deal and collect his $10,000. He can meet Helen at the title office and write her a check for $60,000. She then assigns the mortgage to him and exits the picture. Jim later meets Bob, who has a check made out to Jim for $70,000, and the mortgage is transferred to Bob. Jim deposits Bob's check into his account, and when the check to Helen clears, Jim has his $10,000. This is known as a simultaneous or "double" closing.

Suppose Helen demands a cashier's check, and Jim doesn't have the cash? He could arrange to have Helen and Bob close the deal together, in exchange for a $10,000 "fee" from Bob. Or Jim could simply sell his option on the mortgage directly to Bob for $10,000.

Most states do not require a mortgage broker's license for this kind of deal, since it is considered to be a finder's fee for a mortgage transaction that has previously been entered into public record. Contact your State Banking Commission for current regulations.

One more scenario. Suppose Jim inadvertently over-prices the property and can't find a buyer? If Jim asks $60,000 and the best offer he gets is $50,000, is he $10,000 in the red? Absolutely not. Whenever Jim makes an offer to Helen (or any seller), it is subject to verification of all details relevant to the sale. If Jim gets into trouble, he is well within his legal and ethical rights to cancel the deal, based on his re-evaluation of the property. His only loss would be his non-refundable deposit on the forty-five-day option.

This is why it's so important to accurately determine the value of each property. Real estate is only as valuable as the price someone is willing to pay for it. Stay clear of inflated, over-hyped quotes, and stick to the basics. Focus on motivated sellers, and don't even consider a property that you wouldn't be happy to live in yourself.

Locating Privately Held Mortgages

In order to be successful in paper, you need to be accessible to the right people. Classified ads are an excellent way to do this. All you need is a straightforward ad such as: "Will Pay Cash for Your Mortgage. Call Jim: 555-1234." The word "cash" is the magnet that will attract attention. You can project the image of a high roller even if you're working with little or no money.

But a classified ad will only get the attention of people intending to sell. An excellent place to locate all mortgage holders is the county recorder's office. You'll find an invaluable cache listing every mortgage filed by a bank or an individual. This is the best-kept secret in the paper game.

Here's what you do: drop by the county recorder's office, and ask to see the *mortgagors' index*. This lists the names of banks, credit unions, and private individuals who are currently receiving payments from mortgagors. You're looking for the names and addresses of the mortgagees. Scroll down the list of mortgagees until you spot the name of a private individual, and jot it down. Then look to the left of the name for the corresponding reference number, and refer to the reference book for a copy of the original mortgage document. You now have the name and address of your first prospective seller. Repeat the process to find as many as you need.

The next step is to draft a letter to these mortgagees, introducing yourself as a real estate investor who pays cash for mortgages. Remember, most people are unaware of their options in this area. It's up to you to explain the benefits to them. Draft a sales letter, and encourage them to call you for more information. When the calls start coming in, ask a few questions about the property and mortgage particulars, and tell them you'll get back to them with a quote after you've had an opportunity to assess the property. If it looks good, secure an option and go after prospective buyers. Between 20 and 40 percent of all mortgages in the U.S. are held by private individuals, making the county recorder's office an inexhaustible gold mine, filled with billions of dollars in privately held paper.

The Option Advantage

An option is an agreement between a property owner and a prospective buyer that gives the buyer the right to purchase at a specified price within a certain period of time. An option is only binding to the seller, and the buyer reserves the right of refusal. However, there must be some consideration involved (usually a fee) in order for the option to be enforceable. If the buyer decides not to purchase the property, the seller keeps the fee. If the option is exercised, the fee is applied to the purchase price.

Consideration for an option generally takes the form of a fee agreed upon between the buyer and seller. You can also negotiate a "right of first refusal" option. A right of first refusal gives the buyer the opportunity to match any offer received by the mortgage seller, or to be first in line when the seller decides to sell a specific property.

If you make several deals with the same property owner, you may use a "rolling" option. This means that every time you exercise an option and close a deal, you can get a new option on another property from the same owner.

Always notarize and record all options with the county clerk. Obtain a preliminary title report to verify all information provided by the optioner, and insist that the option be transferable. Always go for the lowest consideration and longest time frame possible. Cover all contingencies in the option, such as insurance, death of the property owner, bankruptcy, loan default, and maintenance of the property. Have your attorney take care of the paperwork so that you'll have more time to focus on day-to-day operations.

Holding Paper

The beauty of paper is that, after just a few transactions, you can reinvest the profits and start holding paper yourself. You'll be receiving monthly payments from mortgagors and

---

POWERTIP

The "One Percent" Rule. Following this rule will guarantee your liquidity if you are holding paper on a property. It means that, in order to break even, you need to receive no less than 1 percent of the purchase price in monthly rent payments. For example, if the property is worth $120,000, you need at least $1,200 in rent each month to avoid negative cash flow.

generating positive cash flow, allowing you to live on the interest and invest the principal.

The Golden Rules of Paper

- Real estate is only as valuable as the price someone is willing to pay for it.
- Only purchase paper on property you would be proud to own yourself.
- Research mortgagees in a variety of county recorder's offices, and keep accurate records of responses.
- Run your classified ads in regional, small- to medium-market newspapers. They are less expensive, and they have a more responsive readership than larger papers.
- Never mail sales letters during tax season or the Christmas holidays.
- Stay on top of current rent and real estate prices; read trade publications.
- Maintain records of the criteria required by investors (buyers).
- Ask prospective paper sellers what they need the money for; you'll gain valuable insight into their motivation for selling and their true wants and needs.
- Follow the One Percent Rule!

Checklist for Real Estate Success

1. Locate sellers through classified ads or through the county recorder's office.
2. Field calls and gather information about the property.
3. Discuss specifics of property and mortgage details with seller.
4. Inform the seller you'll contact him or her with a quote after appraisal.
5. Evaluate the property.
6. Secure a forty-five-day option if you are interested.
7. Contact prospective investors (buyers) through classified ads.
8. Discuss property and mortgage specifics with buyers.
9. Obtain quotes, and establish the best offer.

10. Determine the closing date.
11. Sign a mortgage purchase agreement (MPA) with the seller.
12. Sign the MPA with the buyer.
13. Conduct appraisal, title, credit check, etc.
14. Close the deal!

If you're unfamiliar with real estate, there are plenty of sources at bookstores and libraries on the subject to help you. Remember, knowledge is not only power; it also breeds confidence and success. When you harness the same techniques used by banks and financiers, it won't be long before you achieve a lifetime of wealth and prosperity.

CHAPTER 15

CYBERMARKETING

*The machinery for dreaming
planted in the human brain was
not planted for nothing.*

Thomas De Quincey

CYBERSPACE IS THE INVISIBLE REALM between you and the person with whom you communicate by telephone or computer. The "information superhighway" includes cellular communication, fax, e-mail, and the Internet. In cyberspace you can communicate, access information, exchange ideas, and conduct business. There is a wealth of income potential in cyberspace. Virtually any product can be marketed on this fascinating new frontier where the rules are still being made. As new technologies replace existing ones at lightning speed, the industry remains in a constant state of evolution.

With a new venue for business comes a new vocabulary you must learn. In this chapter you will encounter many unfamiliar terms. For your convenience there is a short Internet glossary at the end of the chapter to introduce you to some of these words.

What Is the Internet?

The Internet is a worldwide interconnection among computers. It includes an estimated 40,000 networks in 135 countries, linking more than thirty million computers through traditional telephone lines. These are ballpark figures; the Internet is too large for a reliable census system, although such companies as A.C. Neilsen and Arbitron are currently searching for ways to quantify it.

The Internet (or "Net," for short) has no borders or governments. Of the twenty-five-million-plus Net users in the U.S., a core of three million spend hours at a time "surfing" online. Forecasts indicate that the Internet will include one billion computers in the near future. It has been estimated that if the aircraft industry had grown as rapidly as the computer industry, the Concorde would now carry 10,000 passengers on a single trip, travel sixty times the speed of sound, and the fare would be less than one dollar per passenger.

AT&T plans to make the Internet available to every home in America. Now you can even access the Net through a special box for your television set. This is an untamed new frontier, self regulated and bursting with inexhaustible opportunity for entrepreneurs.

Perhaps the most explosive avenue is the marketing of books, reports, and newsletters online, since information is the primary reason people use the Internet. Selling specialized and proprietary information is making a growing number of "infopreneurs" fabulously wealthy in a very short period of time. You can get started with very little money, and reach millions of potential customers worldwide.

On the Net, virtually anyone working out of a spare bedroom or garage can compete on equal terms with multinational corporations. Through the Internet, you can reach millions of potential customers more inexpensively than via any other advertising medium, and your overhead costs for mailing lists, printing, postage, fulfillment, and advertising are reduced or eliminated. You can distribute sales literature to prospective customers from electronic mailing lists, post messages on electronic bulletin boards (BBSs), or place an interactive multimedia presentation on the World Wide Web. You can quickly process credit card orders and even download an information-related product.

The majority of Internet users are educated and discerning. If you can provide the information they need and make it easily accessible, there's no limit to the amount of money you can make. The Internet is the most incredible reach vehicle in the history of advertising. Many entrepreneurs have already made their fortunes selling information online, and more will follow. Why not you? For general information about the Internet, contact the Internet Society at (703) 648-9888.

Marketing on the Internet

Advertising on the Internet was forbidden in the early days, since government funding mandated that there be no for-profit activities. Laurence Canter and Martha Siegel, lawyers from Arizona, have the dubious distinction of being the early pioneers of advertising on the Internet. In April of 1994, Canter and Siegel advertised their legal services by flooding the Internet with messages and e-mail (called "spamming"). Despite being flooded with "flames"—obnoxious insults and threats from Internet purists—the duo reportedly attracted some $100,000 in business for less than two hours of work. To this day, Canter and Siegel continue to battle the anti-advertising factions on the Net.

While the introduction of online capitalism was initially greeted with hostility, there's plenty of room for everyone in cyberspace, including honest and responsible "cyber-preneurs." For information on marketing on the Internet, contact:

Internet Business Report
(800) 340-6485, or e-mail: *rob@ost.com*
Small Business Administration on the Web
http://www.sbaonline.sba.gov

For a free newsletter about Internet advertising and publicity, send e-mail to Interactive Marketing Alert: *majordomo@marketplace.com* with the following in the body of the message: "subscribe cyberbiz-I."

To receive information on electronic "cyber-malls"—virtual storefronts where you can advertise your product or service—contact:

> **Branch Information Services**
> (313) 741-4442, or e-mail: *info@branch.com*
> **Global Network Navigator**
> (800) 998-9938, or e-mail: *info@gnn.com*
> **Downtown Anywhere (on the Web)**
> *http://www.awa.com*
> **The Internet Mall**
> *http://www.internet-mall.com* on the Web, or send e-mail containing the message "send mall" to: *taylor@netcom.com*

Don't Let Your Ad Get Lost in the Net

The Internet has been accurately described as a library with no catalog file. The sheer volume of information translates into thousands of winding "dirt roads" on the information superhighway. For "cyberpreneurs," however, it's best to focus on the main thoroughfares. If your ad is not tied to an online publication such as *Wired* or *Internet World,* it can be difficult to find.

The Internet is unlike any existing medium in that, ideally, it is not advertising by intrusion; it's advertising by invitation, and it is almost completely customer-driven. People must access your ad or Web site in order to receive your information. This is part of what makes the Internet such a unique marketing vehicle.

Throughout this chapter, you will discover many ways to publicize your business and target your market in cyberspace. Here are some of the ways to sell products and information on the Internet:

- E-mail
- Electronic mailing lists

- Usenet newsgroups
- Electronic bulletin board systems (BBSs)
- The World Wide Web (WWW)
- Cybermalls
- Classified ads

How to Get Online

In order to access the Internet, you'll need the following:

- A PC with a modem
- Standard telephone service
- Internet service from a local provider or commercial network such as America Online, CompuServe, Microsoft Network, etc.
- An e-mail software program and a Web browser program (if you're not on a commercial network)

For questions about Internet access, contact the InterNIC Help Line at (619) 455-4600.

SERVICE PROVIDERS

Access providers have the powerful computers you need to get connected to the Internet; they are your onramp to the information superhighway. You can get online with either a local service provider or a commercial network. Commercial services such as America Online and CompuServe offer complete Internet packages including e-mail, access to Usenet newsgroups and the Web, chat rooms, message boards, online shopping, and other exclusive services. However, some of these services can be limited or slow and awkward to use.

Local Internet service providers, or ISPs offer direct Internet access, e-mail, and Usenet news, often at a cheaper, flat rate. (In fact, in response to members jumping ship to local ISPs, America Online recently lowered their rates to a flat fee of $19.95 per month for unlimited access.) To hook up through an ISP, call your local service provider, and ask for an Internet account that includes an e-mail address, access to the World Wide Web, and server space so you can post your business's home page on the Web. You'll receive a telephone number to connect your PC to their main computer, and you're on your way.

If you live in an area with a local service provider, you can get on the Internet with a local call. If there is no provider in your area code, you can save on long-distance telephone charges by signing up with either an out-of-state provider that has a toll-free number, or a commercial network that will most likely have a local phone number for your use. If you are not yet online, check the Yellow Pages under "Computer Services Online" to look up ISPs. If you are already online but looking to change your service, check out this Web site that lists about 1,900 service providers by country, state, and area code, as well as individual services and fees: *http://thelist.com.*

Service provider information is also available online from "PDIAL" by sending a message containing the phrase "Send PDIAL" to *info-deli-server@netcom.com.*

A Word About Equipment

Software   Windows-based PCs require a Windows socket, or *WinSock.* Also, ask your service provider for a PPP connection (Point-to-Point Protocol—upgraded technology that makes your PC a point on the Internet, using a high-speed modem and WinSock software). This lets you dial directly onto the Internet, and can cost anywhere from fifteen to fifty dollars per month, depending on your location.

Modem   In order to take full advantage of the Internet, you'll need a speedy modem—one that operates at least 14,400 bytes per second (bps) for data processing. Don't confuse the data-processing speed with the fax speed. A 14,400 bps modem is great, a 28,800 bps modem even better, and ISDN lines are the fastest.

Cost

A basic system that includes e-mail and Internet access costs between twenty and forty-five dollars per month. This includes a certain amount of hourly access time, with a surcharge for additional time.

Your costs will consist of the following:

- Obtaining a link from your service provider
- The necessary hardware and software to operate your Web site (see below)
- Designing and updating data on your site
- Attracting people to your site through links from other sites
- Offline advertising for your site, such as business cards, sales literature, newspaper classifieds
- Additional publicity, such as news releases and postings to chat areas, Usenet News, mailing lists

Info-Docs

Info-docs are the informative documents you'll use to promote your product or service on the Internet. In many areas, such as newsgroups and BBSs, blatant advertising is a no-no. The purpose of your info-doc is first to inform and enlighten, then to direct interested people to your e-mail address or Web server for additional details. You should have three variations of info-docs on disk and ready to upload to appropriate areas of the Internet:

1. A short, five- or six-line "teaser" relating to your industry that will stimulate interest and show people where to find additional information—e-mail, Web server, file transfer protocol (FTP), etc.
2. A one-page report or article about your industry or company, written in the style of an independent report, with a creative slant designed to generate even more interest in you and your business. Remember, testimonials are golden.
3. Your sales literature, including the features and benefits of your product or service, along with prices and ordering details. Keep this to one or two pages, in order to make it easy to download.

To find the people you want to reach with your message online, check out the DejaNews service on the Internet, at *http://www.dejanews.com.*

Sign-Off (SIG)

Avoid any reference to your business in the info-docs and messages you post online. Save this for your sign-off, or SIG. This is the place to provide your name, business name, and e-mail address. Be sure to limit it to three lines, or it may be cut off. You can check your message by posting it to *alt.test* on Usenet. Keep your SIG in a text file for easy copying to the end of all of your online postings. You may want to have two separate e-mail addresses: one to dispense automatic information (called an *autoresponder*) and another for specific questions or requests.

E-mail

Electronic mail is an excellent vehicle for making money on the Internet. Messages sent by e-mail are like regular letters, but they travel between computers electronically through regular telephone lines. E-mail moves much faster than regular mail, or "snail mail." There are no charges for postage or long-distance calling, and you can send e-mail anywhere in the world for next to nothing. Long-distance telephone calls are expensive because they travel directly from point A to point B, whereas e-mail travels through a series of small "hops" between a myriad of computer networks; you only need to pay for a telephone call to the nearest "node."

POWERTIP

Reply.Net is a service that provides businesses with a way to respond to e-mail requests from customers. Your information is sent to prospects within five minutes of the time they sent their inquiry. The cost of this service is fifty-nine dollars per month, plus thirty cents for each message it sends for you. Contact Reply.Net at (800) 210-2220 or (301) 930-3011, or send e-mail to *get.info@reply.net.*

Everyone on the Internet has an e-mail address, assigned by either a local service provider or a commercial network such as America Online, CompuServe, or Prodigy. To the "newbie," e-mail addresses may resemble a foreign language.

When you establish an Internet account, you receive an e-mail address from your access provider. The e-mail address consists of two initial parts: your "login" name (your name or company name), and your "domain" name (which shows where to find you on the Internet through your access provider's main computer). These are separated by an @ symbol. Your login name appears to the left of the @ symbol, and your domain name to the right. If Bob Jones is a subscriber to America Online, the first two parts of his address would be: *bobjones@aol.*

The next part of your e-mail address shows the geographic location or specific activity engaged in by your service provider's receiving computer. The common designations are "gov" for government, "edu" for educational institutions, and "com" for commercial. Therefore, Bob Jones's complete e-mail address would be: *bobjones@aol.com.*

When choosing your e-mail name, remember that the name itself can be a powerful marketing tool. Pick a descriptive title that illustrates what you do, similar to a vanity telephone number or license plate for your car.

Direct E-mail Lists

Mailing lists allow you to communicate with people all over the world about subjects of mutual interest via e-mail. If I send e-mail to the Home Business Marketing mailing list, all the people who "subscribe" to the mailing list will receive a copy of my message in their e-mail in-boxes and can reply

---

POWERTIP

The bi-monthly online newsletter *Accessing the Internet by E-Mail: Dr. Bob's Guide to Offline Internet Access* is available by sending a message to *mail-server@rtfm.mit.edu.* Leave the subject area blank, and in the body of the message write: "sendusenet/news.answers/internet-services/access-via-email."

to my message—either privately or to everyone on the list. This is an exciting and informative way to communicate internationally with people who share your interests.

There are presently more than 100,000 lists of e-mail addresses, covering any topic you can imagine. E-mail lists typically have anywhere from 100 to 500 subscribers, but the number of messages you'll receive from the list on a daily basis will vary. Simply locate an appropriate list and subscribe to it. You'll be automatically added to the list, and you can exchange information with everyone else on the list.

This is like a traditional direct-mail campaign, but there are no costs for postage, printing, coding, or envelope stuffing. Your message must be subtle, and it should follow the thread or topic of the subject matter relating to each list. Sending blatant advertising just isn't worth the flames you'll attract. Remember, subtly put all contact information for your business in your SIG.

To find mailing lists that interest you, start with Rich Zellich's "List of Lists" at: *ftp://sri.com/netinfo/interest-groups.txt.*

LISTSERV COMMANDS

The following commands are used with listserv mailing lists, a current file of e-mail lists. Listserv helps you find the names and addresses of lists, subscribe or unsubscribe to lists, review lists, or change your personal preferences for any list to which you subscribe.

> **SUBscribe**   Subscribe to a mailing list
> **UNSubscribe**   Unsubscribe to a mailing list
> **List**   Receive a list of all the mailing lists at a specific server
> **REView**   Obtain details of a mailing list
> **Query**   Review your optional settings for a mailing list
> **SET**   Change your optional setting for a mailing list
> **CONFIRM**   Confirm your subscription to a mailing list
> **Stats**   Display statistical information about a mailing list

Mass E-mail

Net purists believe that, because the cost of sending unsolicited e-mail is shared by the recipient on his or her e-mail account, their rights are being trampled when they receive e-mailed advertising. They compare getting unsolicited e-mail to interrupting the Super Bowl in the middle of a play to show a commercial.

Recent surveys revealed that approximately 80 percent of people with e-mail accounts don't mind receiving unsolicited mail. A further 10 percent simply send a "remove" message. This leaves a vigilant and angry 10 percent to continue spending more time (and expense) flaming, reporting, complaining, and mail-bombing than it takes to simply delete the offending ad and get on with their lives. Their priorities puzzle me. In fact, "unlimited access" e-mail accounts are common, and provide unlimited use for a flat monthly fee (such as ISPs and America Online). However, there is no mistaking the purists' passion. Regardless, if the statistics are any indication, there's a tidal wave approaching, and—for better or for worse—it will not be stopped.

These two heavily armed camps—the purists and the capitalists—are each determined to impose their will on the other. Until some kind of compromise is reached, perhaps in the form of software that blocks or filters unsolicited e-mail, the war will continue to rage on. The alarming irony is: as this battle over individual rights and freedom escalates, it provides increasing incentive for Big Brother to intervene.

For discussions on all aspects of marketing and advertising on the Internet, subscribe to the INET Marketing mailing list at *inet-marketing@einet.net.*

DIRECT E-MAIL LIST BROKERS

There are hundreds of subscriber lists on the Internet containing specific subject groupings. A good source for list brokers are computer and Internet magazines. Prentice-Hall also publishes a directory of Internet lists. To receive a current file of listserv groups, send an e-mail message to Bitnet at *listserv@bitnic.educom.edu.* Type "list global" in the text of your message and leave the subject area blank.

Usenet Newsgroups

You can find a newsgroup for almost any topic, no matter how bizarre. This is fertile ground for your info-docs.

Newsgroups are accessed with a special program obtained from your service provider. The *biz.misc* category alone has more than 100,000 subscribers. The *alt.* category is also a good place to locate newsgroups in your subject area.

Avoid posting the same info-docs to multiple groups. Today there are "killbots," programs that seek out unwanted messages and remove them from offending inappropriate areas of the Internet. If you're caught spamming, some service providers may cancel your account.

Tailor your messages to blend in with each particular group. The key to marketing success with newsgroups and "chat rooms," is to hang out and "listen" before diving in. Get a feel for the subject matter. Provide information and answer questions pertaining to your area of expertise, then invite interested parties to e-mail you for additional information.

DejaNews offers one of the most popular Usenet search options. You can visit DejaNews on the Web at *http://www.dejanews.com.*

SIFT is a free personalized Usenet filtering service provided by Stanford University that allows you to focus on specific topics and combine them onto a single page. Information is available at *http://sift.stanford.edu.*

Public Usenet News Servers

Usenet news servers are computers that users without a news server can use to read and post to newsgroups. If you don't have Usenet News access, or if you want to gain access to newsgroups that your server doesn't carry, enter one of the following public Usenet news servers in the news preferences box of your browser (you must change your news server preferences in order to use one of these servers):

> *online.magnus1*
> *news.ak.net*
> *news.ichange.com*

Electronic Bulletin Boards

Electronic bulletin board services (BBSs) are accessed by telephone through your computer. There are more than

60,000 BBSs with seventeen million users—four times the total number of subscribers to the commercial online services. This provides an excellent opportunity to reach the groups most likely to be interested in your offer. Many BBSs are privately run by individuals out of their homes or offices. Some BBSs charge a small annual fee, but many are free. Most are "moderated" or screened for content, and disallow blatant commercial messages, although they welcome informative articles or news releases of interest to their subscribers.

The largest BBS in the world is EXEC-PC. Thousands of BBS systems operators (SYSOPs) use it as a primary source of information on new files (articles, news releases, etc.). To place a file on EXEC-PC, dial (414) 789-4360 with your modem. Log on as a guest, go to the file area, and upload your news release or industry business article. It may be picked up by hundreds of other BBS operators, saving you the time and effort of posting to them individually. The location of EXEC-PC on the Web is: *http://www.execpc.com/*.

Another way to get the attention of SYSOPs is to advertise in the magazines they read. *Wired, BBS Magazine,* and *Online Access* are good places to start. For advertising rates and services contact:

BBS Magazine
Callers Digest, Inc.
701 Stokes Road
Medford, NJ 08055

Online Access
Chicago Fine Print, Inc.
900 North Franklin, Suite 310
Chicago, IL 60610
Fax: (312) 573-0520

Wired
Wired Ventures, Ltd.
520 Third Street
San Francisco, CA 94107
(415) 222-6200

World Wide Web

While the Internet is the physical network of interconnected computers, the Web is simply the graphical subset of information that can be accessed by the Internet. The Web is the most exciting growth area on the Internet for marketing products and information. Bursting with cybermalls, virtual storefronts, electronic classified ads, and cutting-edge ideas and technologies, it grew by almost 350,000 percent in 1993. In 1993, just over 1 percent of all Web sites were commercial; by 1995 nearly half of the Web was commercial. There was over $430 million in sales on the Web last year. The Web is your electronic mega-mall—without leases, employees, or overhead, and is definitely the Mecca of the information superhighway.

The greatest attraction of the Web is that it allows anyone to post and retrieve information on the Internet on a global scale. Unlike text-oriented BBSs, the Web is a graphical area, incorporating multimedia files for photographs, sound, animation, and even full-motion video. Information is linked, allowing you to jump around to different areas by simply following preexisting links. Home pages are accessed with a locational tool called a "uniform resources locator" (URL), which is the launching pad for information searches that can take you anywhere on the Internet.

Writing copy for the Web is unlike any other form of advertising. A Web site must include a high volume of interactive information in an attractive format in order to hold the user's attention.

A Web "site" is an introductory area that provides hyperlinks to other Web pages. It can holding anywhere from a few pages up to hundreds of pages of information. A "home page" is an introductory Web page that provides hyperlinks to other Web pages. The first thing you see when you access a Web site is the home page, which includes the contents and instructions on how to access the various features in the site.

There are a number of excellent software programs that make it easy to design your own Web pages. Microsoft's "Internet Assistant" lets Word for Windows read and write files in Hypertext Markup Language (HTML), the universal Web document format. You can download Internet Assistant from Microsoft's FTP site at *ftp.microsoft.com.*

Create "links" to your Web page in a number of other sites, newsgroups, and cybermalls. This makes it easy for people to access your Web site with the click of a mouse. Seek out businesses that are similar to your own, and band together to link sites. The more variety you can offer as a group, the more hits (or visits) everyone will generate. For a fee, NTG International will submit information about your service to hundreds of Web page databases. They also have a public service Web page where you can publicize your home page. NTGI's Web site is located at *http://www.nygcampus.com/ntg/ public.html.*

Yahoo! is a Web directory listing more than 90 percent of all Web sites. Getting your Web page listed with Yahoo! is like getting a free listing in the Internet Yellow Pages. For links to over 440 online shopping centers, check out Yahoo!'s listing at *http://www.yahoo.com/Business_and_Economy/Companies/Shopping_Centers/index.html.*

For a huge list of business resources on the Internet, check out the Business and Economy section of Yahoo!'s Business Resources at *http://www.yahoo.com.*

For online advertising techniques, netiquette, and links to dozens of other Web sites, check out the Internet Advertising Resources Guide at *http://www.missouri.edu/internet-advertising-guide.html.*

Internet Indexes and Search Engines

Having trouble knowing where to begin? Indexes and search engines can help you explore the possibilities on the Web. When you access these pages, they will be able to search for other pages for you if you simply enter a keyword in the space provided.

Alta Vista *http://altavista.digital.com*
Excite *http://www.excite.com*
Hotbot *http://www.hotbot.com*

Infoseek   *http://guide.infoseek.com*
Lycos   *http://www.lycos.com*
Magellan   *http://www.mckinley.com*
Submit It   *http://www.submit-it.com*
WWW Worm   *http://www.cs.colorado.edu/www/*
Webcrawler   *http://www.webcrawler.com*
Web Announce   *http://wwwac.org/WebAnnounce*
Yahoo!   *http://www.yahoo.com*
GNN   *http://gnn.com*

Business Directories

Business directories help you locate products or services on the Web, just like the telephone yellow pages. The largest of these directories is Nynex's Interactive Yellow Pages, containing more than sixteen million entries. These directories are good places to list your business.

Apollo   *http://apollo.co.uk*
Excite Netdirectory   *http://www.excite.com/Subject/*
Galaxy   *http://galaxy.einet.net*
Mckinley's Magellan Internet Directory
http://magellan.mckinley.com
Nynex Interactive Yellow Pages   *http://www.niyp.com*
Starting Point   *http://www.stpt.com*
Virtual Yellow Pages   *http://www.vyp.com*
The Whole Internet Catalog   *http://nearnet.gnn.com/wic/*
Worldwide Yellow Pages   *http://www.yellow.com*
WWW Virtual Library   *http://w3org/hypertext/*
DataSources/bySubject/Overview.html
Yahoo!   *http://www.yahoo.com*
The Yellow Pages   *http://theyellowpages.com*

Making Your Web Presence Known

Thousands of new sites are added to the Web every day. Starting Point and What's New Too are two great places to

POWERTIP

For a list of links to search engines, visit *http://www.yahoo.com/ Computers_and_Internet/World_Wide_Web/Databases_and_Searching.*

announce your new Web presence. What's New is more selective about which new sites it promotes, and it can be one or two weeks before your site is included. What's New Too adds new sites without discrimination. Other new site postings can be found at What's New at Yahoo! and at Netscape What's New. Here's how to find them:

Net Happenings *http://www.midinet/NET/*
Netscape What's New *http://www.netscape.com/escapes/what's_new.html*
What's New *http://www.www.ncsa.uiuc.edu/SDG/Software/Mosaic/Docs/whats-new.html*
What's New Too *http://newtoo.manifest.com*
What's New on Yahoo! *http://www.yahoo.com/new/*
World Wide Web Information *http://info.cern.ch/hypertext/WWW/Clients.html*
Webaholics *http://www.ohiou.edu/webaholics/index.html*
Web Space Providers *http://www.directory.net/dir/servers.html*
Interesting Business Sites on the Web
http://www.rpi.edu/okeefe/rpi.gif
Entrepreneurs on the Web *http://sashimi.wwa.comnotime/eotw/EOTW.html*

Tips for Designing Your Web Site

When designing the documents that will become your Web pages, it's important to balance your creative approach with the technical realities of the Web. This will enable you to construct an efficient site that will pull the maximum number of inquiries, or "hits."

Most modems operate at 14,400 bps, which means that they are capable of handling about 1K (one thousand kilobytes) of data per second. This means that large amounts of data, heavy graphics, and audio/video files may be too time consuming to download for the average computer user. Studies indicate that twenty seconds is the limit most people will wait for a routine task before they become frustrated, indicating that Web pages should not exceed 20K.

Utilize graphics sparingly, using formats that compress pictures (JPEG) and large blocks of color (GIF) without

POWERTIP

Many Web pages include counters that enable users to track the number of visits, or "hits," to the site. Make sure that your agreement with your service provider includes a provision for a counter. Then Internet Audit Bureau will place an icon depicting their logo on your Web page to count the number of hits you receive. Visit their site at *http:// www.internet-audit.com.*

sacrificing quality. If you include large-image files or audio and video clips, install them as separate documents linked to the home page so that they don't interfere with the downloading speed of the page.

Web technology is in a constant state of evolution, with faster and more efficient programs around every corner.

To find design ideas for your Web site, visit the Web Digest for Marketers at *http://www.advert.com/webdigest/ wdfm2.3html.*

The Two-Step Sales Method for the Web

Once your messages are on the Internet, you could receive an avalanche of responses. The two-step method is the best way to convert information into sales.

After you've posted your info-docs in as many places as possible on the Internet, people will usually e-mail you for additional information.

Now you can send your sales material. Include as much information on your product as possible. Remember, the purpose of the Internet is to exchange information first and foremost. Consider getting a *listserver*—an auto-responder mailbot—from your service provider. This lets you automatically e-mail your sales material to anyone who requests it. For information on auto-responders, send an e-mail message to *majordomo@pop.psu.edu,* and include in the body of the message: "get file majordomo-faq."

Once you begin to generate inquiries, follow up with additional information, including ordering information. You can ask customers to forward a check or money order, or you can accept credit cards if you have a merchant account.

> **POWERTIP**
>
> **Online market research.** For about $500, Los Angeles-based M/S Marketing will post a questionnaire about your product or service to a cross-section of people across the country via newsgroups and targeted e-mail messages. For information, see the M/S Web site at *http://www.msdbm.com*.

There are companies that deal specifically with electronic marketers, and can provide the necessary software (see the Resource Directory).

The next step is fulfillment. You can mail your product to customers, or, if you're selling a book, newsletter, or report, you can give them an access code through a system such as *Softlock*. Softlock allows them to download your publication directly from your computer.

Exchanging Money on the Internet

The security of credit card transactions on the Internet is an ongoing issue. Visa and MasterCard recently joined forces to tackle this problem; you can imagine how eager the financial community is to get their fingers into the Internet pie! The current system of accepting credit card orders involves encrypted (coded) messages between the customer and the merchant. Much of the paranoia about exchanging credit card information is unfounded, since it can be just as risky to give this information over the telephone or to a retail store clerk. However, many home-based entrepreneurs rely on toll-free phone numbers or mail order to get around the issue of security on the Net.

Since it's been reported that an estimated 40 percent of consumers do not have credit cards, some companies have turned to "cyberbucks"—special Internet bank accounts used specifically for shopping online. For more information about Internet banking, contact:

Cybercash *http://www.cybercash.com*
First Virtual send e-mail to *apply@fv.com*, or visit their Web site at *http://www.fv.com*

NetCash   send e-mail to *netbank-info@agents.com*
Verisign   *http://www.verisign.com*

Cybermarketing Tips

- Don't send unsolicited junk e-mail.
- Keep flames to a minimum; never post messages asking for money.
- Don't use all capital letters. This is the online equivalent of SHOUTING. Use all caps only for headlines or titles.
- Never return a flame; it's a waste of time and energy. There's no way to completely eliminate flames; it's part of doing business on the Internet. If you inadvertently post to an inappropriate area and are flamed, apologize for the error.

Summary of Guerrilla Cybermarketing Steps

1. Establish a presence on the Internet (e-mail address, WWW server, FTP/Gopher). Review Figure 15.1.
2. Decide how you're going to accept payment (Internet account, credit cards, or 800 number).
3. Get a listserver or auto-responder for e-mail inquiries.
4. Post your info-doc report or article to EXEC-PC (the largest BBS in the world).
5. Post info-docs to appropriate Usenet newsgroups.
6. Subscribe to appropriate e-mail lists, and send your report to everyone on the list.
7. Post info-docs in free Internet classified areas, such as *.forsale* and *.marketplace.*
8. Subscribe to commercial servers (America Online, CompuServe, Microsoft Network, etc.). Place classified ads and post info-docs to appropriate forums and newsgroups.
9. Include your e-mail address in all postings.

POWERTIP

Insurance for your PC. Safeware Insurance offers an affordable, comprehensive policy. For rates and local availability, contact Safeware at (800) 848-3469.

10. Have your Internet service provider help you construct your Web page or ask them to recommend an affordable Web page designer.
11. Link your Web site to as many other Web locations as possible. Join with other businesses in your field.

Best Books About the Internet

Marketing on the Internet by Michael Mathiesen contains a wealth of information and resources, including free Spry

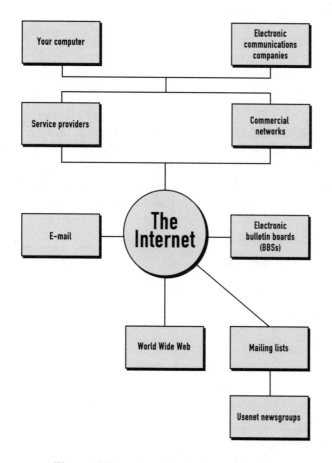

Figure 15.1 *Internet marketing model*

Mosaic software that provides instant access to the Internet. This first edition is 424 pages long, and costs $39.95. Maximum Press is the publisher, and you can contact them at 1501 County Hospital Road, Nashville, TN 37218; (800) 989-6733, code 392. It is also available in the computer section of retail bookstores.

The Whole Internet User's Guide & Catalog by Ed Krol features a user's guide, technical index, and catalog index, and covers all the major user programs, as well as legal and ethical aspects of the Internet. The second edition is 574 pages, and costs $27.95. It is published by O'Reilly and Associates. Contact them at 103 Morris St., Suite A, Sebastopol, CA 95472; (800) 988-9938.

The Internet Yellow Pages by Harley Hahn and Rick Stout contains listings for what's on the Internet and how to find it. The second edition is 447 pages, and costs $27.95. Contact Osborne McGraw-Hill at 2600 Tenth Ave., Berkeley, CA 94710; (800) 822-8158.

The Internet Mailing Lists Navigator for Windows Users by Vivian Neou includes more than 1,400 online mailing lists, do's and don'ts, and free Internet software for automatic list subscription. It costs $39.95, and is available from Prentice-Hall, One Lake Street, Upper Saddle River, NJ 07458.

EntepreneURLs: Cochrane's Favorite Home-Based Business Links

Here is a list of Web sites that will provide a wealth of information about cybermarketing in the home-based business world. General business tips and Internet tips are both available from these sources:

http://www.ro.com/small_business/homebased.html
Small and Home-Based Business Links. One of the best sources of information and resources on the Net.

http://www.copa.ca
COPA: The consumer connection page on this site contains a wealth of helpful hints and product information to help

the small office and home based business entrepreneur. Includes a product locator listing over 1,100 manufacturers and 550 product categories.

http://www.isquare.com
The Small Business Advisor: This award-winning site contains a wide variety of online info for the entrepreneur and small-business owner.

http://www.sbaonline.sba.gov/
Small Business Administration: Excellent resource for small or home-based businesses—full of downloadable articles and software.

http://homeworks.com
Homeworks Home Page: Homeworks regularly updates its site with advice and information for people who are or would like to be their own boss.

http://www.hoaa.com/
Home Office Association of America online.

http://www.tab.com:80/Home.Business/
Home Business Review Magazine online.

http://www.yahoo.com/Business/
Small_Business_Information/
Yahoo!'s links to info for small businesses.

http://www.ibic.com/HomeBusiness/HBICIntro.html
Home Business Information Center, sponsored by the American Home Business Association.

http://web.miep.org/sbfa/
Small Business Foundation of America. The research institute for emerging enterprise.

http://mall.netmar.com/mall/shops/solution/
Home Business Solutions.

http://www.pacificrim.net/~patents/
The Strategic Patent Web Site: A comprehensive guide to patent resources.

http://www.gmarketing.com
Weekly online magazine tailored to small business.

http://home.comm.net/~horizons/
Electronic publisher. Read the electronic books at your computer.

http://www.en-wave.com
The Entrepreneur's Wave: A specialty bookseller catering to small and home-based business owners, start-ups, and self-employed professionals.

http://www.transecure.com
Secure Transactions: This service allows individuals and small businesses to complete secure transactions online. Vendors without secure server capabilities can sell their products online accepting credit cards and more.

http://www.hits.net/~netbiz
Books and More: Internet's largest home-based dedicated bookstore. Books, reports, management system, taxes, audiocassettes, books-on-disk, etc. Over 1,500 titles, 10,000 files, free information, and more.

http://www.bizresource.com
Packed with helpful tips, plus ideas and motivation for business owners. Includes an online entrepreneur's quiz.

http://aimc.com/aimc/
American Individual Magazine and Coffeehouse: Hangout for entrepreneurs and individualists, with Starting a Business and Working from Home Centers.

http://www.webcom.com/~promoent/directory.html
Virtually Free Mall: Free information, services, and items useful to entrepreneurs.

http://members.aol.com/vstation/index.htm
Downloadable online magazine featuring home-based business opportunities and other money-making programs. Place an ad and submit your URL here.

http://www.nae.org/bookstor.html
America's largest collection of entrepreneurial, self-employment and home-based business titles.

http://www.tab.com/Home.Business/YellowPages/
Home Based Business Yellow Pages: New directory of U.S. and Canadian home-based businesses. Add a free listing for your home business.

http://www.ultranet.com/~iw/homebase/list1.htm
The Home Based Business Directory: Mail-order products sold exclusively by home-based businesses. Add your business.

http://www.hotfiles.com
ZDNet. A hot site packed with shareware for business or pleasure.

http://www.owplaza.com/
One World Plaza. Your one-stop worldwide business connection. A wealth of information.

http://www.bizweb.com/
BizWeb. Another prime source.

http://www.catalog.com/impulse/invent
The Invention Store.

http://edgeonline.com/
Entrepreneurial Edge Online. Your one-stop-shop offering the resources, information, research and education necessary to successfully start or grow your business.

http://www.incomeops.com/
Income Opportunities magazine online.

http://catalog.com/corner/
Entrepreneur's Corner Office.

http://www.ahba.com
The American Home Business Association online.

http://www.gohome.com
Business@Home online Magazine. Their motto is "Making a life while making a living."

http://www.ggold.com
Global Gold's Home Business Site. Excellent tips and resources!

http://magnet.mwci.net/mall/relonet/biz-web/intro.html
Home-Based and MLM Bizweb.

http://www.ultranet.com/~iw/homebase/dir.htm
Home-Based Business Directory.

http://www.tab.com/Home.Business/
The Home Business Review. A monthly online newspaper designed to "educate and promote the nation's home based businesses by providing business building articles, information, and resources. All of the articles are written at the 'how-to' level instead of just theory, providing a 'news you can use' approach."

http://www.homeworkers.com
The International Homeworkers Association. "Helping People Prosper in the Home Workplace."

http://www.newwork.com/
Brave NewWork World. Information, ideas, opinion, advice, continuing work education, and a range of interesting, entertaining content through a variety of media, helping you prepare for the new millennium.

http://www.usahomebusiness.com/homesite.html
National Association of Home-Based Businesses online.

http://www.hoc.com/
Home Office Computing online.

http://www.eotw.com/index.html
Entrepreneurs on the Web. One of the top sites for information, resources, and helpful links.

http://www.csupomona.edu/ace/
Association of Collegiate Entrepreneurs, California Polytechnic University, Pomona.

http://www.netaccess.on.ca/entrepr/
Entrepreneur Online (not the magazine).

http://www.commerce.net/
A superb resource for information on how to conduct business on the Internet.

gopher://una.hh.lib.umich.edu/00/inetdirsstacks/ cyberpren%3aschwilk
Cyberpreneurs Guide to the Internet. Listings of newsgroups, BBSs, etc.

http://www.vidya.com/add-lib/
Vidya's Guide to Internet Advertising. A free resource for Web publishers and promoters, with up to date listings of free and "pay" advertising opportunities on the Web. Here's where you'll find appropriate sites, and people offering ad space to announce yourself to potential sponsors.

The Internet Glossary

Browser   The client software that runs on your desktop PC, enabling you to browse the Net. Examples include Netscape Navigator (the current market leader), Mosaic, Eudora, and Microsoft Internet Explorer.

Cybermall (electronic mall)   Online storefronts that provide a cyberspace where multiple business sites are hosted.

Cyberspace   Term for the online community; be it the Internet, Web, or a commercial online service such as America Online, CompuServe, Prodigy, or the Microsoft Network.

FAQs   Frequently Asked Questions, a routine way of presenting answers to commonly asked questions to people browsing the Web.

Flame   Abusive e-mail, often caused by a failure of the recipient to observe the rules of "netiquette."

GIF   The standard graphics file format of the Web, recognized by all browser software.

Hit   An individual instance of a person logging in to a particular page in a Web site at a particular time.

Home button   An icon that returns you to a site's home page from wherever it is positioned within the site.

Home page   The main point of entry, or URL, for a Web site. Often contains a table of contents.

Hypertext   Text-based data that is "linked" across multiple documents or locations.

HTML   Hyper Text Markup Language for electronic publishing, the specific standard for the World Wide Web.

HTTP   Hyper Text Transfer Protocol, the actual communications protocol that enables Web links and other features. Every Web address begins with "http"; think of it as the "area code" for the Web.

Imagemap   A single Web image in which individual bits are "mapped" to their respective positions, enabling variable mouse-driven control by clicking on different areas of the image.

Interactive   Two-way communications of an ongoing nature as opposed to delayed interaction, as with e-mail. Chat rooms and Internet phones are examples of interactive communication in cyberspace.

IRC   Internet Relay Chat, the Internet's live chat area for online conferencing.

JPEG   A standard graphics file format on the Web and in electronic publishing. An alternative to GIF files.

Link   The connection between two information objects or two Web sites.

Listserv   One of the three main listserver programs that automate mailing lists on the Net. The other two are *listproc* and *majordomo*.

Mailbot   An automated agent that responds to e-mail queries and sends a predetermined message based on a set of criteria.

Netiquette   The unwritten rules of the road on the information superhighway.

Newbie   A rookie, or novice, Internet citizen. We all start out as newbies.

Post   To place or publish a message or file to a newsgroup or Web site.

Internet service provider (ISP)   A commercial vendor that sells connections to the Internet, and related services to organizations seeking a Net presence.

Spam   To post advertising messages in any area of the Web or newsgroup where they are unwelcome.

TCP/IP   Transmission Control Protocol/Internet Protocol. The standard Internet procedures that handle traffic and define how data is formatted, labeled, and routed.

Toolbar   A bar-shaped graphic image, usually placed at the top or bottom of a page, to provide a convenient, context-sensitive command menu.

URL   Uniform Resource Locator, or Internet Web address. Begins with *http://* followed by, for example, *www.mywebsite.com*.

Webmaster   The principal author or publisher at a particular Web site.

World Wide Web   The graphical subset of information that's available on the Internet.

PART FOUR

Protecting Your Assets

CHAPTER 16

FINANCIAL FLOURISH: KEEP YOUR BANKER FROM ROBBING YOU BLIND

> *Establish a society in which the individual has to pay for the air he breathes (air meters; imprisonment and rarefied air), in case of non-payment simple asphyxiation if necessary (cut off the air).*
>
> **Marcel Duchamp**

Most people encounter money problems because they see cash solely as the means with which to maintain their lifestyle. The fact is, if you spend your money as fast as it comes in, no matter how much you earn, *you will never achieve financial independence.* You must shed your old spending patterns and develop a practical new way of looking at money. Refocus your priorities: invest first, spend second.

Reframing Your Belief Systems

Despite the good intentions of our parents and other early role models, most of us have been fed a steady diet of baloney since childhood. We've been cajoled, wheedled, and brainwashed into believing that the only way to achieve happiness and security is to:

1. Get a good education
2. Find a good job
3. Get a mortgage, buy a house, pay the bills, and invest what we can for a rainy day

Ask yourself a simple question: how many of the people who taught you everything you know about money are wealthy right now? Becoming the master of your financial destiny actually involves more *unlearning* than learning.

Let's start with education. I believe that education serves only one purpose: it can open doors and lead to contacts. Rarely, however, does education teach you the street skills you need to survive in the real world. The best way to obtain the knowledge you need is from experts who have succeeded in the real business world. This information is readily available to anyone who desires it.

We were told that "a penny saved is a penny earned," and other conservative yarns destined to confine us to a life of mediocrity. Risk was for the irresponsible, the dreamers. The fact is, no one ever accomplished anything of significance in life without risk. Here's another fable: "money is the root of all evil." On the contrary. It's a statistically proven fact that the dark side of humanity is revealed more often in deficiency and despair than in prosperity. The hopelessness caused by financial hardship is the single dominant factor in social dysfunction, domestic abuse, and violent crime.

The sooner we unlearn these damaging belief systems, the more quickly we can make the transition from deficiency motivation to prosperity consciousness. This is the single most important step on the road to financial and emotional well-being. In order to transform your financial mind-set, you must decide that not having financial independence will be more painful than the effort and commitment required to achieve it.

Make financial independence the top priority in your life. Become a student of wealth; absorb everything you can and use your experiences as a tool with which to forge your destiny. Embrace the things that work, and discard those that don't. Develop relationships with professionals, such as an accountant, attorney, or broker, who have a vested interest in helping you succeed. Their expertise will pay for itself a thousand times over. You don't have to be a know-it-all, but it is your responsibility to ask the right questions. Decide today. Right now.

Why do you want to be financially secure? What will your life be like five years from today if you don't do anything? Start with the why, and the how will look after itself. The subconscious mind is a powerful thing. It sounds mystical, but it really works. When you absolutely and irreversibly decide to go for it, refusing to accept anything short of total success, you'll be astonished by the speed at which things begin to fall into place. Your subconscious mind actually goes to work on the problem to help you find the answers.

We've been taught to pay our bills first, provide a comfortable lifestyle for our family, and sock away what's left in savings. Think about that for a moment. According to this so-called wisdom, by the end of each month we'll have paid everyone except ourselves. Aren't we at least as significant as the mortgage lender, car dealership, credit card company, and other faceless entities that compete for our hard-earned dough? Instead of relinquishing our economic power, we must learn to harness it in the form of leverage, savings, and investments.

The moment you decide that you rank at least as high as your creditors, your focus instantly shifts from merely scraping by every month to investing in leverage (using your money to make more money). Focus on your financial resources instead of what you lack. Stop procrastinating and stressing out, and start looking for effective, enjoyable ways to create value and prosperity. This is the most important step you can take toward providing a secure future for yourself and your loved ones.

There are two separate but equally effective modes for creating wealth: active and passive. Building wealth using your personal resources to develop positive cash flow is *active*. Making your money grow through leverage, savings, and investments is *passive.* Passive wealth multiplies itself continuously, even while you sleep. Recognize the difference between elements that are within your control (positive, consistent financial habits) and those that are not (inflation, interest rates, etc.) Otherwise, the greatest money-making opportunities and financial planning in the world will be useless.

After all, it isn't what you earn that makes you wealthy, it's what you *keep.* Making more money is not the answer. Bad spending habits will make twice as much money disappear twice as fast. Consider the number of wealthy athletes and entertainers who blew their fortunes because they failed to grasp these fundamentals. One of the most dangerous myths is that making more money will automatically make you rich.

If you don't even read the other information in this book, you can become a millionaire using the money you already have. This means managing your money, instead of allowing it to manage you. Get out of debt, and stay out of debt. Use this chapter to form a plan of attack to make your money work for you, and stick with it. Heck, it's only your *future* on the line! Dump that passbook savings account and look into higher-yield instruments such as mutual funds. Don't be intimidated. According to the Investment Company Institute, 25 percent of all Americans own mutual funds, and you can start an account for as little as twenty-five dollars a month.

It may seem like many of the tips that follow are too petty or inconsequential to worry about. Bankers count on this attitude. It translates into billions of dollars in profits from the legalized skimming of your money. Why just accept this treatment when a little extra attention to detail

---

POWERTIP

The Ten Percent Rule. If you do nothing other than save 10 percent of your total income every month for the next ten years, you will be rich. Not only will you have a year's salary, you'll also have captured the indomitable power of compound interest.

can get your money working for you, instead of for the brazen financial monolith that plunders your assets and jeopardizes your family's security and future?

Five Simple Steps to Taking Control of Your Budget

1. Calculate your total income.
2. Prioritize your expenses into categories.
3. Set your budget limits.
4. Write everything down, and control your cash flow.
5. Look for ways to make your disposable cash earn more (leverage).

It's easy to make excuses for not investing. The most common excuse is not having enough disposable income to make it worthwhile. Consider this: if you had a twenty-dollar bill to invest, what would you do with it? By simply putting it toward outstanding credit card debt, at between 18 and 22 percent interest, you would effectively be investing that money at 20 percent. Of course, you're still swimming in negative cash flow. The solution? *Avoid all debt.*

Nothing will keep you from financial independence like outstanding debt. We have become a live-today-pay-tomorrow society. The shrewd entrepreneur knows that this is a sucker's bet. This attitude is what makes it possible for the financial infrastructure to legally embezzle more than $100,000 from the average person over the course of his or her lifetime. Your money should be working for you, not for your bank. If you absolutely must borrow, go short term and double up on the payments whenever you can. Shop around and negotiate the best possible terms. Even one extra point can make a sizable difference in interest charges.

If you have a few thousand dollars in a savings account earning a paltry 6 percent, you're wasting that money by not investing it. There's no need to go off the deep end. Just set aside what you need for security and invest the rest. There are several effective ways to do this. Offshore accounts are an excellent non-taxable investment instrument. Ask your broker or financial advisor for more information. Retirement plans (IRA, 401(k), Keogh) continue to rank among the most powerful tax shelters around, multiplying your investment while diverting taxes until age fifty-nine and a half.

Consistently invest in your business through leverage and by maintaining low overhead. Since the majority of your expenses are tax-deductible, you'll be spending money to make money. Always look for ways to expand your operation. Consider bringing in partners for a 12 to 15 percent return on their investment. They make a profit while you do most of the work, and you can launch your business without risking as much of your own capital.

Using the Financial Infrastructure to Your Advantage

Make no mistake: your bank is poised to shake you down with outrageous interest fees, penalties, and charges on practically every service it provides—from mortgages, credit cards, IRA deposits, and checking accounts all the way down to your child's savings account. Let's examine the common traps and the ways to minimize or avoid their effects, redirecting the balance of power to make the system work for you.

MORTGAGE MANEUVERS

Selecting a mortgage solely on the basis of affordable monthly payments is a recipe for disaster. Over the average thirty-year term, you'll end up paying upwards of $400,000 for a $100,000 property. Why would you want to repay four dollars for every dollar you borrow?

Here's how to turn the tables. First, negotiate a monthly payment you can accelerate without overextending your budget. Increasing your monthly payments by as little as 4 percent can ultimately lead to savings of 25 percent or more over the full term of the mortgage. This can shorten the length of your mortgage by a whopping ten years. Ignore your accountant's advice to go long term for the tax savings. Invest this money for your benefit, not the bank's.

Avoid the adjustable-rate mortgage (ARM) like the plague. This is one of the biggest scams in the business. The adjustable rate is nothing more than a ploy to allow banks to collect maximum interest, regardless of the current rate. Since bankers control the rates, you can always count on the rates to fall more slowly than they rise. For example, if your ARM is based at 11 percent and rises to 13 percent, your increase is not 2 percent, but 20 percent. On a $100,000 mortgage, this could add a few hundred dollars to your monthly payment. Unless you're certain that you will unload the property prior to a hike in interest rates, refuse the ARM and go with a fixed-rate mortgage.

You've probably seen one of the many commercials advertising home equity loans, or credit lines. This is merely a new twist on the same old game—the second mortgage. The few tax advantages are easily devoured by outrageous fees for application, appraisal, credit check, and so on. Again, you end up paying back two dollars for each dollar borrowed. Your home equity should be reserved for genuine emergencies, since it's your last line of defense against foreclosure.

INTEREST RATE RUSES

Let's look at some of the devious tricks banks teach their loan officers, in order to pad interest rates by an additional quarter to half percent. Perhaps your greatest disadvantage is that the majority of negotiations occur on the banker's home turf—his or her office. Whereas the average borrower might negotiate a loan or mortgage only a few times, the banker does this routinely. Prepare for the appointment beforehand, and bring up interest rates early in the proceedings. The loan officer will try to deal with everything else first, and then ambush you with the rate after you're hooked. Here are several ways this might be done:

- The officer announces, "the rate on this particular loan is X percent." Don't buy it. Unless it's a small consumer loan, there's always room for negotiation.
- "In order to put the deal to bed as soon as possible, let's go with an X percent rate for the time being, and we'll get

back to it later. "They're betting you won't get around to bringing it up later, and you can bet they won't.

- You are treated to a tap dance about how "when weighed against the cost of equity capital, finance, or secondary mortgage rates, this rate will be a bargain after taxes." No, it won't.
- The banker doesn't even bother to mention the rate, quickly scribbling it into the contract and hoping that you won't notice or care.

CREDIT CARD CARNAGE

You might be surprised to learn that Visa, MasterCard, and American Express don't actually issue credit cards; they only process charges and payments on the cards. Banks license the credit card name and set interest rates and fees themselves. The fact that you receive your card from a small bank doesn't necessarily mean that you'll be getting the lowest rate. Small banks are merely agents for the larger issuing banks. In fact, Visa has approximately 1,500 issuing banks, compared to almost 11,000 agent banks nationwide. The bottom line is that one Visa card may be remarkably different from another, depending on the issuing bank.

A loophole in federal law exempts out-of-state banks from usury laws limiting the rate of interest and fees an issuing bank may charge on its credit cards. This explains the increase in direct, aggressive consumer solicitation. You should be extremely skeptical about responding to offers for "a guaranteed Visa or MasterCard." There can be a substantial variation in terms and fees, even within your home state.

Pay attention to the fine print. Most banks do not charge interest on balances from purchases until you are billed. If the bill is paid in full by the due date, there is no interest charge. Banks make their killing in carryovers, in which the customer carries an outstanding balance from month to month. This is where you're looking at 18 to 22 percent interest. Some banks begin charging interest from the moment they receive the charge slip and make payment to the billing merchant. Here, the interest meter is running even before you receive the bill. Other cards are billed on a twenty-four-day cycle, with customers receiving fourteen bills per calendar year. If you usually pay your bills once a month, any one of those fourteen could easily slip through, costing you interest on the balance and maybe even appearing on your credit record as a "late payment."

Many banks advertise interest-rate "specials" that might look good on the surface, but revert to a higher rate after the promotion expires. If you decide to take advantage of these promotions, beware of the expiration date, and be prepared to switch banks if necessary.

Another efficient way to tip the scales in your favor is to take a cash advance on your credit card, and pay for goods and services with the cash instead of charging them. Interest charges on cash advances can be 5 or 6 percent lower in some cases. If you are being charged a higher rate for goods and services, use the cash advance to switch the balance to a lower rate. Keep in mind that interest on cash advances accrues from the day the money is withdrawn, so be sure to time the cash advance one or two days before the bill becomes past due before you pay off the merchandise purchases. You'll find this date on your schedule of services and fees from the issuing bank. Also, watch out for transaction charges on cash advances—they can be steep!

Negotiating the "Float Moat"

"Float" refers either to the time between your date of deposit and the date when the bank allows access to those funds, or the period of time between when you make a payment and when that payment is credited to your account. Most people overlook the potential leverage of float. Banks don't. In fact, they are earning $50,000 a year from the free use of your money as you read this. Turn the tide by using a bank with a reasonable "hold" policy toward deposit accounts. The simple difference between a hold policy of three calendar days and three business days on a standard account with an average balance of $4,000 can mean the difference between annual earnings of $220 and no earnings at all. Ask your bank to explain its hold policy.

Make Sure Your Bank Is Solvent

Before you trust your life savings to any financial institution, you should be satisfied with their stability. Start by asking for a copy of their semiannual financial statement. Check the bank's net worth and look for any unusual recent spurts in loan activity; this could be a tip-off of an overextended bank. Determine whether they are diversified as opposed to focused on a single area.

Most financial institutions are required to publish an accountant's report, which is a good way to check for discrepancies with the financial statement you've received. If you have $100,000 or more invested in the bank, you are entitled to full access to their investment portfolio. Despite reports that the banking industry is on an upswing, more than 650 banks (about 5 percent) are still in a state of financial stress. Choose a bank that has equity in excess of 5 percent of its assets; 4 percent after deducting loans in excess of reserves.

Money Secrets of the Wealthy

- Pay off your mortgage as soon as possible.
- Put discretionary capital—money just sitting in the bank collecting minimal interest—to work.
- Weigh every purchase on a cost/benefit basis.

POWERTIP

Faster Check Clearance
- Always make sure the check is endorsed.
- Make sure the check is not post-dated, and that the written dollar amount matches the numerical amount.
- Deposit checks before 2:00 p.m.
- Ask your bank about electronic direct deposit. Checks deposited this way are usually available the same day.
- Don't make deposits through an ATM (automated teller machine). Checks deposited this way could take an extra day or two to clear—maybe longer if the ATM is not owned by your bank.

- Participate in an automatic transfer from your bank account to a mutual fund.
- Predetermine how much money you need to make it through life's expenses (college tuition, medical emergencies, etc.).
- Don't go into debt to pay for assets that have little or no value.

How to Eliminate 100 Percent of Your Debt and Live on Cash

As consumers, we've been manipulated and misled to believe that we can have everything we need today, with little thought to true cost. We're exposed to a barrage of advertising encouraging us to "Buy now! No payments or interest for ninety days!" Then there's "Visa . . . it's everywhere you want to be"—if where you want to be is the poorhouse!

We've become a nation of runaway impulse buyers. We spend money before it's earned, and mortgage our futures to the financial infrastructure through grossly inflated interest rates and service charges, just for the "privilege" of getting in over our heads.

Interest rates on mortgages cost two to three times the amount of the principal over the full term. Credit card rates are well over 20 percent. Every dime of interest due is money that you must eventually earn. We've become shackled to insurmountable debt, enslaved to banks and financial institutions and the economy they control. This subservience is the root of many of society's ills—unemployment, bankruptcy, divorce, depression, alcoholism, and crime.

The Big Lie is everywhere. Accountants advise us to never pay off the mortgage because of the "tax advantages." Where's the logic in paying a dollar of interest just to save twenty-eight cents in tax deductions? A $100,000 home costs three times its value over an average thirty-year term.

Car loans are just as bad or worse, since interest rates are comparatively higher because of the shorter term. You can bet that if banks could find a way to pull off a twenty-year "auto mortgage" they'd do it in a flash! A new car depreciates by several thousand dollars the moment you drive it off the lot. A $22,000 car with a five-year loan might be worth $4,000 after five years, if you're lucky. Never go into debt to buy anything that depreciates in value.

This doesn't mean that you have to drive a jalopy. You're about to discover how to beat the system by eliminating 100 percent of your outstanding debt and operating strictly on a cash basis. And you'll do it more painlessly and efficiently than you've ever thought possible.

Start by reframing your attitudes toward credit and its actual impact on your life. The only thing credit does is inflate the cost of everything you buy. Why mortgage your tomorrow and fill your today with stress and anxiety just for the short-term gratification of having a few things now? It's time to regain control by learning to effectively manage compound interest with powerful strategies that will allow you to:

- Get rid of all your outstanding debt (including your mortgage)
- Function entirely on a cash basis
- Invest your nest egg and make it grow
- Choose a comfortable lifestyle and enjoy your financial freedom

Begin by calculating how much of your monthly disposable income is tied up in credit payments. If 70 percent of your net (after-tax) income is swallowed up by credit payments and you're living on just 30 percent of your income, how can you possibly get ahead? As you reduce your debt load, your net income will increase proportionately. This creates powerful leverage that allows you to pay off larger debt, including your mortgage. People have progressed through this cycle in five years or less.

When you're debt-free, you live on 100 percent of your income. Your main expenses are reduced to bite-sized incidental bills (phone, utilities, tax, etc.), and you discover the invigorating power of cash. You'll routinely enjoy substantial discounts and savings of between 25 and 60 percent on almost everything you buy, new and used. Discounts replace surcharges (interest rates and other "time-payment" fees). When you pay cash, you're truly free. You'll never worry about your credit rating again, because it will be irrelevant. Instead, you'll enjoy the indescribable exhilaration of knowing you've beaten the system!

I know, you're thinking that while all of this sounds great, you won't be able to come up with the money to actually make it happen. There are no smoke and mirrors involved. When you sit down and examine your budget, you'll be amazed at how much fat it contains. *It's possible to accelerate your payments and eliminate debt using as little as 10 percent of your monthly income.*

For example, if your monthly net is $2,000, you'd start with $200. Make a list of all your outstanding debts, including both the outstanding balance and the monthly payment for each. For each debt, divide the balance by the monthly payment to see how many months it will take you to pay it off. Now list all of your debts, in descending order, from lowest to highest total amount owed. Start the process by paying off the lowest debts first, working your way down the list.

The next thing to do after you've made your list is to cut up your credit cards. This is crucial. Keep just one credit card for roadside emergencies. Did you realize that paying off a credit card debt that has interest charged on the outstanding monthly balance yields a return equal to investing funds in an interest-earning account at the same rate? Even as interest rates fluctuate, every dollar you put toward prepaying a credit card at 20 percent interest earns a guaranteed after-tax return of 20 percent. Read that again. This is why it's impossible to effectively invest money while simultaneously carrying outstanding credit debt. It's a no-win deal—just another part of The Big Lie.

Credit lulls us into a false sense of security by dulling our natural purchase-resistance instincts. When you consider the consequences of each purchase (how many hours you'll have to work to pay the full price plus interest), you'll be more likely to make rational, responsible decisions.

You'll be amazed how easy it is to trim the fat from your present budget once you examine the habits that are killing you. You don't need a brand new car. Extended warranties are unnecessary. Are you paying for comprehensive insurance you'll never use? Stick to basic coverage. Instead of going out, plan fun evenings at home with homemade pizza and videos. There are plenty of books on effective cost cutting, but it's mostly common sense. Focus on one area of debt elimination at a time. Many people have successfully unloaded their small debt in one year, then used the money once chewed up by car payments and charge accounts to take dead aim at their mortgage. You can become completely debt-free in five years or less.

Don't worry about saving or investing until you've eliminated all of your outstanding debt, or you're putting the cart before the horse. Earning 3 percent on your savings while paying 21 percent in interest is voluntary extortion. You need all of your available capital working for you.

Don't look at this as deprivation; you're actively regaining positive control over your finances and emotional well-being. Visualize yourself owning your own home. You'll gain plenty of inspiration from the knowledge that you're taking the bull by the horns and creating a lifetime of financial security for yourself and your loved ones.

SUMMARY OF STEPS TO TOTAL DEBT ELIMINATION

1. List all outstanding debt (monthly payments and total balance).
2. Arrange outstanding amounts in order, from highest to lowest.
3. Divide each total balance by the monthly payment.
4. Destroy all credit cards.
5. Allocate 10 percent of monthly after-tax income to paying off small debt.
6. Pay off debt, beginning with the lowest amount.
7. Increase payments toward larger debt as monthly budget increases.
8. Pay cash and pay *less* for everything you buy!

How to Get a Triple-A Credit Rating in Sixty Days

Start by obtaining a copy of your credit report from one the following major bureaus:

Associated Credit Services
624 E. North Belt, Suite 400
Houston, TX 77060

CBI/Equifax
P.O. Box 4091
Atlanta, GA 30302

TRW
505 City Parkway West
Orange, CA 92667

Trans Union
444 North Michigan Avenue
Chicago, IL 60601

The fee is approximately ten dollars. If you have recently been denied credit because of negative information reported by one of the bureaus, you are entitled to a free copy of your report from that bureau. Include your name, address, date of birth, and social security number. When you receive the report or reports, take the following steps:

1. Address any negative notations on your record. Check for inaccuracies, and ask the bureau to delete them. If your record shows non-payment or late payments, you have two options:

   - You're entitled to submit a maximum 200-word statement explaining the circumstances of the information in your file. Don't make excuses; indicate that you were not at fault, that you always pay your bills on time, and that perhaps there is a clerical error or oversight.
   - If you have an outstanding balance, negotiate a settlement with the creditor whereby you agree to repay all or part of the debt in exchange for their agreement to change the notation in your record to a positive, such as "current account" or "paid satisfactorily." Draft a letter outlining the terms of the repayment agreement, and make sure that it is worded correctly and signed by the respective parties *before* you pay.

2. Open an account at a large national bank such as Bank of America or CitiCorp. Large banks carry more weight with credit bureaus than do credit unions or savings and loans.
3. Make a deposit of between $500 and $3,000 to that national bank, and obtain a secured credit card using your deposit as collateral.
4. Repeat this procedure at two or three different banks, using funds from the credit card obtained from the previous bank.
5. For sixty days, make the minimum payments on each card before interest accrues.
6. After you've demonstrated your good credit by making payments on time, the banks will begin to increase your credit limit and offer you an unsecured card. Choose the best card, use it to pay off all the others, and you will have Triple-A credit!

THE DAWN OF
A NEW DESTINY

> *The credit belongs to those who are actu-
> ally in the arena, who strive valiantly;
> who know the great enthusiasms, the great
> devotions, and spend themselves in a
> worthy cause; who at the best, know the
> triumph of high achievement; and who,
> at the worst, if they fail, fail while daring
> greatly, so that their place shall never be
> with those cold and timid souls who know
> neither victory nor defeat.*

Theodore Roosevelt

ONE THING SHOULD BE crystal-clear to you by now: there are more ways to market and promote an idea or product than there are hours in the day! You know where and how to target thousands or even millions of prospects. The resources and amazing techniques of the pros are at your fingertips. You can easily customize an unbeatable business plan, tailored to your present financial means. Use all the information that pertains to your interests, and make your program as potent as it can be. Seize the moment, embrace it, and keep it close to you every day.

There can be no excuses. It's time for a plan of action. Inspiration and a game plan are useless without commitment—and commitment is an ongoing process that must be regularly fed through actions. Choose the path that excites you, and hit the trail! There's a world of prosperity waiting for you to stake your claim. Write down your goals. If you don't know where you're going, how will you know when or if you get there? Here's a simple exercise to get the ball rolling:

1. Write down your goals.
2. Write down why you want to accomplish those goals.
3. Ask yourself the price of achieving your goals.
4. Resolve to do whatever it takes to pay that price.

Take the consistent actions that will guide you toward your dreams. Order books or tapes and attend seminars—whatever you need to motivate yourself each and every day and to eliminate negative and defeatist emotions. Remember, you'll see it when you believe it.

Success is like a snowball. It starts out small, but begins to develop momentum as you go. Drop me a line and let me know how you're doing. I'd love to hear your comments and suggestions.

One final thought: as the wealth begins to flow, remember that the level of thinking that got you where you are will never be the same level of thinking that will get you to the next plateau. Irving Berlin said, "The toughest thing about success is that you have to keep on being a success." The road to prosperity is a journey, never a destination. Embrace the journey, and cherish your freedom.

I wish you health, success, and contentment.

—Patrick Cochrane

RESOURCE DIRECTORY

PROVIDED HERE are some of the best resources for kitchen-table entrepreneurs. Categories are listed alphabetically; use bookmarks, flags, and highlighters to mark resources that will be helpful to you.

Advertising and Publicity

Advertising Age
Crain Communications
740 North Rush Street
Chicago, IL 60611

Weekly trade magazine covering advertising in magazines, trade journals, and business.

Bacon's Newspaper/Magazine Directory; Broadcasting/Cable Yearbook
Bacon's Information Service
332 South Michigan Avenue, #900
Chicago, IL 60606
(800) 621-0561
Fax: (312) 922-3127

Also available from Bacon's Information Service is *Bacon's Publicity Checker,* a source used by many public relations firms.

Directory of Newspapers and Periodicals
Gale Research Company
835 Penobscot Building
Detroit, MI 48226
(800) 877-4253

Print Media Placement
Audiotext News
2362 Hempstead Turnpike, Second Floor
East Meadow, NY 11554
(516) 735-3398

Contains alphabetical listings for 200 newspapers in forty-nine states, as well as advertising rates, circulation, addresses, and restrictions on 900 numbers (if any). $49.95; updates annually.

**Standard Directory of
Advertising Agencies**
National Register Publishing
Reed Reference Publishing
Company
121 Chanlon Road
New Providence, NJ 07974
(908) 464-6800

Working Press of the Nation
National Research Bureau
225 West Wacker Drive, #2275
Chicago, IL 60606
(800) 456-4555

Source for newspaper, magazine, radio, television, and
feature writers.

Auction Consignment

Anka Company
40 Freeway Drive
Cranston, RI 02920
(800) 556-7768
Fax: (401) 567-2159

Bar Code Printing Services

Fotel
(800) 834-8088

General Graphics
(800) 887-5894

International Artwork Service
(415) 969-2403

Catalogs

Catalog Age
6 River Bend Center
P.O. Box 4949
Stamford, CT 06907
(203) 358-9900

The Catalog of Catalogs
1020 North Broadway,
Suite 111
Milwaukee, WI 53202
(414) 272-9977
Also available in bookstores.

Catalogs Worldwide
Interstate Publications
P.O. Drawer 19689
Houston, TX 77224

Free publication containing
listings for hundreds of
catalogs.

**The National Directory
of Catalogs**
Oxbridge Communications, Inc.
150 Fifth Avenue
New York, NY 10011
(800) 955-0231

Over 800 pages, packed with
thousands of catalogs including address, contact, product
line, circulation, and general
information. Includes tips on
selling to catalog houses.
$225; updated annually.

**The U.S. Government
Information for Business Catalog**
Superintendent of Documents
Stop SM
Washington, DC 20401
Fax: (202) 512-1656
Web site:
http://www.access.gpo.gov/sudocs/

Direct-Mail Co-ops
(see also Mail Order/
Direct Mail)

Money Mailer, Inc.
15472 Chemical Lane

Huntington Beach, CA 92649
(714) 898-9111

Money Stretchers
6799 Parma Park
Cleveland, OH 44130
(216) 842-9080

Treasure-Pak, Inc.
2228 28th Street
St. Petersburg, FL 33813
(800) 237-8895

Trimark
184 Quigley Boulevard
New Castle, DE 19720
(302) 332-2143

Electronic Marketing

Electronic Retailing
7628 Densmore Avenue
Van Nuys, CA 91406
(818) 782-7328

**National Infomercial
Marketing Association (NIMA)**
1201 New York Avenue NW,
Suite 1000
Washington, DC 20005-3917
(800) 962-9796

Operations & Fulfillment
magazine
535 Connecticut Avenue
Norwalk, CT 06854
(203) 857-5656

Practical solutions for
direct-response operations
management. $36 annually
for six issues.

Response TV
201 East Sandpointe Avenue,
#600

Santa Ana, CA 72707
(800) 346-0085, ext. 477

Magazine of the direct-
response and infomercial
industry. Excellent source of
ads for fulfillment, commercial production, consultants,
and telemarketing companies.
$39 annually for twelve issues.

**Steven Dworman's
Infomercial Marketing Report**
11533 Thurston Circle
Los Angeles, CA 90049

Exhibit Display

The Godfrey Group, Inc.
P.O. Box 90008
Raleigh, NC 27675
(919) 544-6504
Fax: (919) 544-6729

Nomadic Display
7400 Fullerton Road
Springfield, VA 22153
(800) 732-9395

**Professional Exhibits and
Graphics**
3104 O Street, #341
Sacramento, CA 95816
(916) 498-1183
Fax: (916) 446-8944

Fair and Trade Show Promoters

Amusement Business
P.O. Box 24970
Nashville, TN 37202
(800) 999-3322

Features listings of state and
county fairs.

Bill Communications
P.O. Box 888
Vineland, NJ 08360
(800) 266-4712

A two-year listing of over 7,000
trade shows and exhibitions in
eighty-two different industries.

Fair Times
P.O. Box 692
Abington, PA 19001

Marketer's Forum
Forum Publications
383 East Main Street
Centerport, NY 11721
(516) 754-5000

Information about flea market
publications.

Successful Meetings magazine
Directory Department
633 Third Avenue
New York, NY 10017

Trade Show Bureau
1660 Lincoln Street,
Suite 2080
Denver, CO 80264
(303) 860-7626

Trade Show Week Data Book
(800) 521-8110

Lists over 4,000 consumer and
trade shows covering 104
industries.

Trade Shows Worldwide
(800) 347-4253

*Home Business
Organizations*

Business Ship/Business Kids
One Alhambra Plaza,

Suite 1400
Coral Gables, FL 33134
(800) 282-5437

Books and audiotapes that
teach youth about entrepre-
neurship.

Home Business Institute
P.O. Box 301
White Plains, NY 10605
(914) 946-6600

Home Business News
12221 Beaver Pike
Jackson, OH 45640
(614) 988-2339

Bimonthly magazine.

Home Incorporated
900 East Lafayette Street,
P.O. Box 17148
Baltimore, MD 21233
(410) 223-2678

A range of expert advice on
home business, including tax
tips, money management, and
improving cash flow.

**Home Office Association
of America**
(800) 809-4622
Web site: *http://hoaa.com*

**The Independent Business
Alliance**
(800) 450-2422

Offers group medical and
business insurance, merchant
status, loans, legal and
accounting services, telecommunications (including 800
numbers), and discounted
office supplies and services.
A one-year membership costs
forty-nine dollars.

**Mothers' Home Business
Network**
P.O. Box 423
East Meadow, NY 11554
(516) 997-7394

**National Association for the
Cottage Industry**
P.O. Box 14850
Chicago, IL 60614
(312) 472-8116

Publishes the bimonthly
newsletters *Mind Your Own
Business at Home* and *The Kern
Reports,* focusing on trends in
home business.

**National Association for the
Self-Employed**
2121 Precinct Line Road
Hurst, TX 76054
(800) 827-9990

**National Association of
Home-Based Businesses**
P.O. Box 362
10451 Mill Run Circle,
Suite 400
Owings Mills, MD 21117
(410) 363-3698

Home Office Assistance for the Disabled

**Apple Worldwide Disability
Solutions Group**
(800) 732-3131

**IBM Special Needs
Information Referral Center**
(800) 426-3333

Home Shopping Networks

The Home Shopping Network
11831 30th Court North
St. Petersburg, FL 33716
(813) 572-8585

QVC
1365 Enterprise Drive
Westchester, PA 19308
(800) 345-1515

Income Opportunity Publications

*Business Opportunities
Handbook*
1020 North Broadway,
Suite 111
Milwaukee, WI 53202
(414) 272-9977

*Entrepreneur/New Business
Start-ups*
2392 Morse Avenue
Irvine, CA 92714
(714) 261-2083

Extra Income
734 Monte Drive
Santa Barbara, CA 93110
(805) 569-1363

Income Opportunities
1500 Broadway
New York, NY 10012
(212) 642-0627

Money Making Opportunities
11071 Ventura Boulevard
Studio City, CA 91604
(818) 980-9166

Opportunity
18 East 41st Street
New York, NY 10017
(212) 376-7722
Fax: (212) 376-7723

Small Business Opportunities
1115 Broadway
New York, NY 10010
(212) 807-7100

Spare Time Magazine
5810 West Oklahoma Avenue
Milwaukee, WI 53219
(414) 543-8110

Success
230 Park Avenue
New York, NY 10169
(212) 551-9500

Letterhead, Business Sets, and Paper Products for the Home Office

Great Papers
(800) 287-8163

Image Street
(800) 462-4378

Montage
(800) 482-4626

Paper Access
(800) 727-3701

PaperDirect
(800) 727-3701

Queblo
(800) 523-9080

Viking
(800) 421-1222

Invention Marketing

The American Manufacturers Directory
American Business Directories
5711 South 86th Circle
Omaha, NE 68127

The Dream Merchants
2309 Torrance Boulevard,
Suite 201
Torrance, CA 90501
(310) 328-1925

Trade magazine for inventors.

Thomas' Register
Thomas Publishing Company
One Penn Plaza, 26th Floor
New York, NY 10119
(212) 695-0500

Mail Order/Direct Mail (see also Direct Mail Co-ops)

The Complete Mail Order Sourcebook
John Wiley & Sons
605 Third Avenue
New York, NY 10158
(800) 225-5945

By John Kremer; paperback:
$19.95.

Direct Mail List Rates & Data
Standard Rate & Data Service
3004 Glenview Road
Wilmette, IL 60091
(800) 851-7737

Direct Marketing Magazine/ Friday Report
Hoke Communications

224 Seventh Street
Garden City, NY 11535
(516) 746-6700

Weekly newsletter covering
mail-order and direct-mail
marketing, as well as the latest
legislative and postal news.
$165 per year.

Directory of Mail Order Catalogs
Grey House Publishing
Pocket Knife Square
Lakeville, CT 06039
(800) 562-2139

Lists over 7,000 catalogs.

Directory of Mailing List
Companies
Todd Publications
18 North Greenbush Road
West Nyack, NY 10994
(800) 747-1056

Fees: $45 biannually.

The Do-It-Yourself Direct Mail
Handbook
Marketer's Bookshelf
402 Bethlehem Pike
Erdenheim, PA 19038
(215) 247-2787

By Murray Rafhael and Ken
Erdman; $19.95.

Inside the Leading Mail
Order Houses
Maxwell Sroge Publishing, Inc.
731 North Cascade Avenue
Colorado Springs, CO 80903

The Mail Order Product Guide
B. Klein Publications
P.O. Box 6578
Delray Beach, FL 33482
(561) 496-3316

Lists over 1,500 manufacturers
and distributors that are
looking to sell their product
by mail order.

The Mail Order Business
Directory
B. Klein Publications
(see above)

Contains over 12,000 of the
most active mail-order and
catalog houses in the U.S.,
distributing several hundred
million catalogs annually.
Listed by categories, names of
buyers or executives in
charge, phone numbers, sales
volume, and products carried.
Also contains over 1,000
leading Canadian and foreign
mail-order companies. In-
cludes a concise guide to
selling to the mail-order
market. Ninety-five dollars for
the 500-page, 1996 edition.

Mail Order Legal Guide
by Erwin J. Keup
Oasis Press
300 North Valley Drive
Grant's Pass, OR 07526

National Mail Order
Association
207 Polk Street NE
Minneapolis, MN 55418
(612) 788-1673

Provides affordable help for
small businesses that market
through mail order. Membership fee includes subscription
to *Mail Order Digest* (merchandising methods, marketing
plans, mailing list sources,
and more).

National Mail Order Classified
P.O. Box 5
Sarasota, FL 34230

Write for a free package of discount classified and display ad rates in a variety of high-pulling magazines.

The National Marketplace
Interstate Enterprises
P.O. Box 19689
Houston, TX 77224

Excellent discounts on classified and display advertising in newspapers, magazines, and card decks. Send $1 for a catalog.

Zip
401 North Broad Street
Philadelphia, PA 19108

Industry magazine for direct mail, including lists, fulfillment, etc.

Mail-Order Magazines for Best Response

American Legion Magazine
700 North Penn Street
Indianapolis, IN 46206

Cappers/Grit
1503 SW 42nd Street
Topeka, KS 66609

Jackpot/National Shopper
P.O. Box 6547
Jacksonville, FL 32236

National Enquirer/Star
600 East Coast Avenue
Lantana, FL 33464

Parade
750 Third Avenue
New York, NY 10017

Popular Science
380 Madison Avenue
New York, NY 10017

USA Weekend
535 Madison Avenue
New York, NY 10022

Marketing

American Marketing Association
310 Madison Avenue
New York, NY 10017
(212) 596-8110

Direct Marketing Association
11 West 42nd Street
New York, NY 10036
(212) 206-1100

Direct Selling Association
1776 K Street NW, Suite 600
Washington, DC 20006
(202) 293-5760

Dun & Bradstreet Sales and Marketing Information Catalog
Dun & Bradstreet
Information Services
3 Sylvan Way
Parsippany, NJ 07054
(800) 624-5669

Free list of the names and addresses of over ten million businesses.

Target Marketing
North American Publishing
401 North Broad Street

Philadelphia, PA 19108
(215) 238-5300

No B.S. Marketing Newsletter
Empire Communications
5818 North 7th Street, #103
Phoenix, AZ 88014
(800) 223-7180

Merchant Accounts for Home-Based Businesses

Merchant Services, Inc.
231 Quincy Street
Rapid City, SD 57701
(800) 888-4457

Teleflora Credit Line
12233 West Olympic Boulevard
Los Angeles, CA 90064
(800) 325-4849

Tri-Star International
P.O. Box 51698
San Jose, CA 95151
(408) 345-2365

Card Service International
(800) 735-4171

Newsletters

Newsletters-In-Print
Gale Research Company
835 Penobscot Building
Detroit, MI 48226

Newsletter Publishers Association
1401 Wilson Boulevard, Suite 207
Arlington, VA 22209
(703) 527-2333

Oxbridge Directory of Newsletters
Oxbridge Communications
150 Fifth Avenue, Suite 636
New York, NY 10011
(212) 741-0231

Research/Reference

LEXIS-NEXIS
Mead Data Central
P.O. Box 933
Dayton, OH 45401
(513) 865-6800

Data retrieval from over 1,000 newspapers, wire services, and trade publications.

SCORE (Service Corps of Retired Executives)
National SCORE Office
Small Business Administration
409 Third Street, Suite 500
Washington, DC 20416
(202) 205-6762

Small Business Administration/Small Business Answer Desk
(800) 827-5722
Fax: (202) 205-7064

Washington Researchers
2612 P Street NW
Washington, DC 20007
(202) 333-3499

Retail

Sheldon's Retail
B. Klein Publications
P.O. Box 6578
Delray Beach, FL 33482
(407) 496-3316

Considered the most accurate and complete directory of buyers for major department stores and specialty stores in the U.S. and Canada. Includes addresses, phone numbers, contacts, sales volume data, and more; $145 for the 1996 11th edition.

Self-Publishing

Directory of Syndicated Features
Editor & Publisher
11 West 19th Street
New York, NY 10011
(212) 675-4380
Fax: (212) 929-1259

Infopreneurs: Turning Data Into Dollars
John Wiley & Sons
605 Third Avenue
New York, NY 10158
By Skip Weitzen; $17.95.

Publishers Marketing Association/Audio Publishers Association
2401 Pacific Coast Highway, #102-A
Hermosa Beach, CA 90254
(310) 372-2732
Fax: (310) 374-3342

Essential resources and ideas for the self-publisher. Includes a newsletter and comprehensive resource directory.

Looking Good in Print: A Guide to Basic Design for Desktop Publishing
Ventana Press
P.O. Box 2468

Chapel Hill, NC 27515
(919) 942-0220
By Roger C. Parker; $23.95.

Publisher's Weekly
R. R. Bowker Magazine Group
Cahners Publishing
249 West 17th Street,
Sixth Floor
New York, NY 10011
(212) 645-0067

Weekly magazine covering the book publishing industry. How to find agents and publishers, plus guidelines, tips, etc. Other titles from R.R. Bowker: *Literary Marketplace, International Literary Marketplace, Publishers' Trade List Annual, American Book Trade Directory, Ulrich's International Periodicals Directory* (lists 120,000 magazines and newsletters). Call or write for a catalog.

Writer's Digest
9933 Alliance Road
Cincinnati, OH 45202

Monthly magazine for writers. Tips, ads for subsidy publishers, and literary resources. Write for subscription rates.

The Writer's Guide to Book Editors, Publishers, and Literary Agents
Prima Publishing
P.O. Box 1260
Rocklin, CA 95677
(916) 632-4400

By Jeff Herman; call for the 1997–98 edition. Also available in bookstores.

Short-Run Book Printers

C&M Press
(303) 375-9922

McNaughton & Gunn
(313) 429-5411

Patterson Printing
(800) 887-5894

Thomson-Shore, Inc.
(313) 426-3939

State Press Associations

Alabama Press Association
Commerce Center, Suite 100
2027 First Avenue N
Birmingham, AL 35203
(205) 322-0380

Arizona News Association
711 Missouri Street, #119
Phoenix, AZ 85014
(602) 277-3600

Colorado News Association
The Press Building
1336 Glenarm Place
Denver, CO 80204
(303) 571-5117

Florida Press Service
336 East College Avenue, #103
Tallahassee, FL 32301
(904) 222-6401

Georgia Press Association
Georgia Press Building
1075 Springs Street NW
Atlanta, GA 30309
(404) 872-2467

Idaho News Association
117 South Sixth
Boise, ID 83701
(208) 343-1671

Illinois Press Service
701 South Grand Avenue W
Springfield, IL 62704

Indiana Press Association
300 Consolidated Building
115 North Pennsylvania
Avenue
Indianapolis, IN 46204
(317) 637-3966

Iowa Newspaper Association
319 East Fifth Street
Des Moines, IA 50309
(515) 244-2145

Kansas Press Association
5423 Southwest Seventh Street
Topeka, KS 66606
(913) 271-5304

Kentucky Press Association
332 Capitol Avenue
Frankfort, KY 40601
(502) 223-8821

Louisiana Press Association
680 North Fifth Street
Baton Rouge, LA 70802
(504) 344-9309

Missouri Press Association
Eighth and Locust
Columbia, MO 65201
(314) 449-4167

Montana News Association
1900 North Main, Suite C
Helena, MT 59601
(406) 443-2850

Nevada Press Association
P.O. Box 137
Carson City, NV 89702
(702) 882-8772

New England Press Association
(Includes CT, MA, ME, NH, RI, VT)
281 Huntington Avenue, Box 77
Boston, MA 02115
(617) 437-5610

New Jersey Press Association
206 West State Street
Trenton, NJ 08608
(609) 695-3366

New Mexico Press Association
117 Richmond NE
Albuquerque, NM 87196
(505) 265-7859

New York Press Association
Executive Park Tower
Albany, NY 12203
(518) 482-0400

North Carolina Press Association
Raleigh Building, #1100
5 West Hargett Street
Raleigh, NC 27601
(919) 821-3348

North Dakota News Association
222 North Fourth Street
Bismarck, ND 58501
(701) 223-6397

Ohio Newspaper Association
1225 Dublin Road
Columbus, OH 43215
(614) 486-6677

Oklahoma Press Association
3601 North Lincoln
Oklahoma City, OK 73105
(405) 524-4421

Oregon News Association
7150 Southwest Hampton
Portland, OR 97223
(503) 684-1942

South Carolina Press Association
1417 Calhoun Street, Box 11429
Columbia, SC 29211
(803) 254-1607

South Dakota Press Association
Communications Center
S. Dakota State University
Brookings, SD 57007
(605) 692-4300

Tennessee Press Service
1345 Circle Park
Knoxville, TN 37996
(615) 974-5481

Utah Press Association
467 East Third South
Salt Lake City, UT 84111
(801) 328-8678

Virginia Press Association
P.O. Drawer C-32015
Richmond, VA 23261
(804) 798-2053

West Virginia Press Association
101 Dee Drive, Suite 200
Charleston, WV 25312

Washington News Association
3838 Stone Way
Seattle, WA 98103
(206) 634-3838

Wisconsin News Association
702 Midvale Road

Madison, WI 53705
(608) 238-7171

Wyoming Press Association
710 Garfield, Suite 248
Laramie, WY 82070
(307) 745-8144

*Trademark Research
Companies*

Trademark Express
(800) 776-0530

**Trademark Research
Corporation**
(800) 872-6275

Thomson & Thomson
(800) 692-8833

U.S. Border Patrol

Central Office
Detroit, MI
(313) 266-3260

Northeast Office
Buffalo, NY
(716) 846-4101

Southeast Office
Miami, FL
(305) 651-2253

Southwest Office
San Diego, CA
(619) 428-7321

Western Office
Tucson, AZ
(602) 629-6871

U.S. Department of Defense

Region One
Defense Reutilization and
Marketing
926 Taylor Station Road
Blacklick, OH 43004
(614) 692-2114

Region Two
Defense Reutilization and
Marketing
2163 Airways Boulevard
Memphis, TN 38114
(901) 775-6417

Region Three
Defense Reutilization and
Marketing
P.O. Box 53, Defense Depot
Ogden, UT 84401

*U.S. General Services
Administration (GSA)*

GSA Central Mailing Lists
Building #41
Denver Federal Center
Denver, CO 80225

Region One
John W. McCormick
Post Office
Suite 806
Boston, MA 02109

Region Two
230 Dearborn Street
Chicago, IL 60604
(312) 353-6045

Region Three
75 Southwest Spring Street
Atlanta, GA 30303
(404) 221-5133

Region Four
525 Market Street
San Francisco, CA 94105

Region Five
819 Taylor Street
Fort Worth, TX 76102

Venture Capital Organizations

Atlantic Venture Partners
801 North Fairfax Street
Alexandria, VA 22314
(703) 548-6026

Canada Opportunities Investment Network
Ontario Chamber House
2323 Yonge Street, Fifth Floor
Toronto, ON
Canada M2P 2C9
(800) 387-8943

Georgia Capital Network
ATDC
430 Tenth Street, Suite N-116
Atlanta, GA 30318
(404) 894-4543

Heartland Capital Venture Network
1710 Orrington Avenue, Suite 22
Evanston, IL 60281
(312) 864-7970

International Venture Capital Institute
P.O. Box 1333
Stamford, CT 06904
(203) 323-3143

Investamerica Venture Group
600 East Mason Street
Milwaukee, WI 53202
(414) 276-3839

Iowa Venture Capital Network
2700 College Road, Box 4-C
Council Bluffs, IA 51502
(712) 325-3437

National Venture Capital Association
1655 North Fort Meyer Drive, Suite 700
Arlington, VA 22209
(703) 351-5269

Northwest Capital Network
P.O. Box 6650
Portland, OR 97228
(503) 294-0643

Private Investor Network
University of South Carolina at Aiken
Aiken, SC 29801
(803) 648-5851

Southeast Venture Capital Funds
One Southeast Financial Center, Suite 1166
Miami, FL 33131
(305) 375-6470

Venture Capital Network of New York
P.O. Box 248
Lake Placid, NY 12946
(518) 564-3227

Quest Ventures
555 California Street, Suite 2955

San Francisco, CA 94104
(415) 989-2020

Seed Capital Network
8905 Kingston Pike, Suite 12
Knoxville, TN 37923
(615) 693-2091

**Western Association of
Venture Capitalists**
300 Sand Hill Road
Building 2, Suite 190
Menlo Park, CA 94025
(415) 854-1322

Women Venture
2324 University Avenue West,
Suite 200
St. Paul, MN 55114
(612) 646-3808

Wholesale Merchandise Suppliers

Anchor Accessories
P.O. Box 3958
North Providence, RI 02911

The B&F System, Inc.
3920 West Walker Boulevard
Dallas, TX 75236

Mail Order Associates
120 Chestnut Road
Montvale, NJ 07654

The Mellinger Company
6100 Variel Avenue
Woodland Hills, CA 91367

National Wholesale Company
158 Bloomingdale Street
Chelsea, MA 02150

**Specialty Merchandise
Corporation**
9401 De Soto Avenue
Chatsworth, CA 91311

Wholesalers/Import/Export

A Basic Guide to Exporting
U.S. Superintendant of
Documents
(202) 512-1800

Closeout News
728 East Eighth Street, Suite 1
Holland, MI 49423-3080
(616) 392-9687
Fax: (616) 394-0102

Trade magazine for the
wholesale and closeout
merchandise industry. Subscription rate: $55 annually.
Single issues also available.

**National Customs Brokers
and Forwarders Association
of America**
One World Trade Center,
Suite 1153
New York, NY 10048
(212) 432-0050

Information on doing
business abroad, from
regulations to financial
and legal concerns.

World Trade Institute
One World Trade Center,
Suite 55-W
New York, NY 10048
(212) 435-3161

900 Number Information (see also 900 Number Service Bureaus)

Marketing Your 900 Number: A User Friendly Guide
Audiotext News
2362 Hempstead Turnpike,
Second Floor
East Meadow, NY 11554
(516) 735-3398

Excellent resources and tips on advertising, free publicity, press releases, infomercials and media advertising. $39.95.

National Association of Informative Services
(202) 833-2545

900 Know-How: How to Succeed with Your Own 900 Number Business
Aegis Publishing
796 Aquidneck Avenue
Newport, RI 02842
(401) 849-4200;
(800)828-6961

By Robert Mastin; considered to be the bible of the 900-number industry. $19.95.

Telecom Made Easy: Money-Saving, Profit-Building Solutions for Home Businesses
Aegis Publishing (see above)

Telephone products and services designed to make a small business look and sound like a large one. $19.95.

900 Number Service Bureaus (see also 900 Number Information)

Alaska Audiotext
Anchorage, AK
(907) 344-5599

Alert Communications
Los Angeles, CA
(213) 254-7171

American Telecom
San Diego, CA
(619) 283-5500

Ameritech Audiotext
Chicago, IL
(312) 906-3130

Amnex Interactive
New York, NY
(212) 619-1717

Astral Communications
St. Paul, MN
(612) 639-1550

Audio Communications
Las Vegas, NV
(702) 221-5100

Audiotext Communications
Miami, FL
(305) 932-2884

Celebration Systems
Houston, TX
(713) 995-2400

Compu-Call
Toronto, Canada
(416) 594-0939

E-Fax Communications
Oakland, CA
(510) 836-8931

Ideal Dial
Denver, CO
(800) 582-3425

Infoline Technology
Columbus, OH
(614) 885-4636

Instant Information
Boston, MA
(617) 523-7636

InterNet, Inc.
Pittsburgh, PA
(412) 571-3350

ITI Marketing
Cincinnati, OH
(513) 563-8666

Message Technologies
Atlanta, GA
(800) 868-3684

Micro Voice
Minneapolis, MN
(800) 553-0003

National Tel-Tech
Scottsdale, AZ
(602) 274-6444

Neo Data
Dallas, TX
(214) 871-5588

Nortel, Inc.
Provo, UT
(801) 578-8008

Northwest Telco
Reno, NV
(800) 279-0909

Phone Base Systems
Vienna, VA
(703) 893-8600

Telecall, Inc.
Wilmington, DE
(302) 633-3000

Telecomputer Corporation
Washington, DC
(800) 872-8648

Tele-900
Philadelphia, PA
(215) 246-3444

Voice Express, Inc.
Tulsa, OK
(918) 583-8080

INDEX